SOPs ToolBox
Non-profit management tools
community mobilization techniques
practical project management techniques

MANAGING NON-PROFIT

A Practical Guide to NGO and Project Management

By
Iqbal Shah

"A Practical Guide to NGO and Project Management"

Written by
Iqbal Shah

COPYRIGHT

Copyright © 2020 protected

All rights reserved in all media.

DEDICATION

I dedicate this book to my beloved younger brothers Mr. Sharif Khan and Mr. Israr Khan and my loving sister (Nusrat Ara) who proved a guiding torch in writing this book. Thanks brothers and sister for such a wonderful, caring, loving and thought provoking relationships.

left blank

Table of Contents

"A Practical Guide to NGO and Project Management":	1
COPYRIGHT:	2
Preface:	13
Introduction:	17
CHAPTER ONE:	19
Category of NGOs	20
Mutual Benefit NGO:	20
Public Benefit NGOs:	21
Types of NGO	21
Operational NGOs:	21
Advocacy NGOs:	22
Characteristics of NGO	22
No bureaucratic hierarchy and functionality	22
Altruism	22
Voluntarism:	22
work towards raising the standard of living	23
Tying up people with line departments:	23
Classification of NGOs	23
INGO	24
National NGOs:	24
CBOs (Community Based Organizations:-	24
History and Evolution of NGOs	25
Modern NGOs - historical perspectives:	25
The role of NGOs in community development	26
Community:	27
Development:-	27
Community development	27
See Diagram No 1 below.	28
The role of NGOs in community development:	29
Diagram No 2(understanding community development)	30
Registering an NGO	30
Development of Vision and Mission statements	31
Developing aims and objectives	31
NGOs Bylaws Development	31

CHAPTER TWO — 33

- Project Cycle Management (PCM) — 33
- Diagram No 3 (project definition): — 34
- Defining Project — 35
- Project Cycle Management: — 36
- Project Cycle: — 36
- From problem state to the desired state of affairs — 36
- Characteristics of Project Cycle Management: — 40
- Problem Identification Phase: — 41
- Diagram No 8, PCM (Identification Phase): — 42
- Appraisal Phase of PCM: — 43
- Diagram No 9, from appraisal to proposal development: — 43
- Diagram No 10, PCM (Appraisal phase): — 44
- Project financing Phase: — 45
- Diagram No 11, PCM (financing phase): — 45
- Project Implementation and Monitoring Phase: — 46
- Diagram No 12, PCM implementation phase: — 47
- Project Evaluation Phase: — 48
- Types of evaluation: — 48
- Mid-term Evaluation: — 48
- Post-ante Evaluation: — 48
- Diagram No 13, PCM, phase evaluation: — 49
- Main Characteristics of PCM: — 60
- Definition of Logical Framework: — 61
- Community Mobilization — 62
- Community mobilizing and organizing: — 65
- Difference between community mobilization and organization — 65
- Community Development — 68
- Understanding community development — 68

Chapter 3 — 72

- Participatory Approaches to Community Development: — 72
- Participatory Approaches: — 72
- Sustainability factor and people' participation: — 72
- Different participatory techniques: — 73
- Participatory Learning and Action: — 73
- Diagram Mobilization /participatory tools and techniques — 74
- Modern day challenges and community mobilization — 75
- Diagram No 3, comparison; — 78
- UMBRELLA TOOLS AND TECHNIQUES — 79
- Participatory Approaches to Community Development — 79
- Sustainability factor and people participation: — 80
- Different participatory techniques: — 80
- Community involvement: — 80
- Participatory Learning and Action: — 81
- Community Mobilization Techniques: — 81
- Philosopher Socrates technique of people motivation — 83
- Experiential Learning Cycle (ELC) Definition — 84
- Reflecting on Experience — 84
- PIAPS Technique: — 86
- Definition of PIAPS — 86

Types of problems:	86
Primary	86
Secondary:	86
Tertiary:	86
Purpose of PIAPS:	87
Application of PIAPS:	87
PIAPS Diagram	87
TOTE MODEL and its application	88
Problem to desired state of affairs	89
TOTE MODEL	89
The TOTE Model Diagram	90
Motivating peoples using NLP Model	91
NLP Model Motivating People)	90
Motivating people using NLP Logical Model:	90
Defining NLP:	91
Explanation of NLP	91
Purpose of NLP	92
Application of NLP	92
Community Assessment using NLP Model	93
Seasonal Calendar:	94
Defining Seasonal Calendar	94
Seasonal calendar relevance to the project:	94
Seasonal Calendar Diagram	95
RRA (Rapid Rural Appraisal):	96
Characteristics of RRA:	97
Application of RRA	99
RRA Digram	99
Problem Tree/Web:	100
Pre-requisites	101
Problem Tree/Web:	101
Cause and Effect Relationship:	102
Problem Tree/ Cause and effect relationship	103
Questionnaire Method:	104
Understanding the questionnaire method:	104
Characteristics of the questionnaire method:	105
Interview:	107
Interview process Diagram:	108
Village Baseline Survey (VBS):	109
Defining VBS	109
Purpose of VBS	109
Characteristics of Village Baseline Survey:	111
VBS Diagram	112
Need Assessment Survey:	113
Need Assessment Survey	113
Definition of NAS	113

Purpose of NAS	113
Need Assessment Survey Digram	114
CHAPTER FOUR:	**115**
NGO financial management:	115
NGO financial management	115
Characteristics of Good Finance Practices	115
Account System:	117
Internal audit	117
External audit	117
Diagram No 38, Internal and external Audit:	118
Diagram No 39, Petty cash terminology explained:	121
Purchases and Procurement:	122
Diagram No 40, Procurement process:	124
NGOs Account and Book Keeping:	124
A good accounting system ensures:	124
Systems of Accounting for NGOs:	124
Types of Accounting Systems:	126
Diagram No 41, Accounting Accruals:	127
2. Accruals Accounting:	128
Bank Reconciliation Statement:	129
Cash Book	130
Bank Book	131
Employees Advance Salaries and Loan Record	131
Pay Roll Sheet	132
Bank Deposit and Withdrawal Record	133
Petty Cash Vouchers	134
Pay Slip	135
Employee salary Sheet	135
The Chequebook Register	136
Salary Certificate	136
Petty Cash Custodian Certificate	137
Petty cash Request	138
Petty Cash Reimbursement Request	138
Petty Cash Journal	139
Petty Cash Reconciliation	139
Salary advances register	140
Advance Salary Request Form	142
Loan Control Register	143

A Practical Guide to NGO and Project Management

Standing Order for Staff Salaries	144
Standing Order for Office Rent	144
Standing Order for Staff Salaries	145
General ledger	146
Fuel voucher	147
Fuel Voucher	148
Cheque Book Dispatch Register	148
Cash Disbursements Journal	150
Payment Voucher	151
Salary Receipt	151
Pay Slip	152
Bank Statement Reconciliation	153
Bank Reconciliation Statement	154
Cheque book register	155
Credit usage Log/Register	155
Fixed Assets Record	156
Petty Cash Transaction Register	157
Bank Statement Reconciliation	157
Balance Sheet	158
Cash Flow Statement	159
Budget Monitoring report	160
Credit memo	161
Notice of dishonored cheque	162
Depreciation method	163
Accounts receivable ledger	164
Aging of Accounts Payable	165
Income and Expenditure account	166
Project Budget worksheet	167
CHAPTER FIVE:	168
Non-profit / NGO Administration:	168
Responsibilities of Administration Department:	168
profit/ NGO Standard operating procedures	169
Employee duty schedule	170
Overtime Form (Excel Sheet)	171
Absence Report	172
Petty cash Request	173
Petty Cash Reconciliation	174
Payment Voucher	174
Petty Cash Custodian Certificate	175
Petty Cash Journal	176
Trucker's LogBook	176
Vehicle log Book for the driver	177
Travel Authorization form	178
Vehicle Schedule of Field Trips	179
Equipment Repair Form	179
Vehicle repair log	180
Equipment sign in and sign out Sheet	181
Vehicle Accident Report	182
Vehicle accident ----------------continued page 2	182
Accident/ incident follow up sheet	183
Purchase Order	184

Purchase Order	**185**
Purchase Order	**185**
Quotation Records (excel Sheet)	**187**
Comparative bid statement analysis	**188**
Supply Requisition slip	**189**
Supply Requisition slip	**189**
Requisition of parts for the maintenance and repair of vehicle	**190**
Request for Quotation	**190**
Supply inward record	**191**
Assets inventory/ assets record register	**192**
Asset Register (A4 Landscape paper)	**193**
Delivery Receipt Form	**194**
PaymentVoucher	**195**
Confirmation of goods (Materials) Received	**196**
Guest book (Visitor book)	**196**
Goods Received Note	**197**
Goods Inspection and Return Report (GIRN)	**198**
Handing over & Taking over of vehicle	**199**
Issue log (excel)	**200**
Request for opening account for new employee	**200**
Loss and damage report	**201**
Register of letter dispatched (a4 landscape or excel sheet)	**202**
Register of Letter Received (A4 landscape or Excel Sheet)	**203**
Staff Movement Register	**204**
Personnel emergency record	**205**
Meeting Agenda/ Purpose	**206**
Previous meeting issues	**207**
Suggestion Form	**207**
Driver's inspection report	**208**
Hotel booking requisition	**209**
Loan Application Form	**210**
Salary advances and loan register	**211**

Assignment Change Request	212
Employee status form	213
Claim for Damage	214
Employee FactSheet	215
CHAPTER SIX	216
Non-profit / NGO logistics:	216
Definition of logistics: Logistics	216
Logistic Management Diagram	217
Drivers and vehicle record	218
Drivers and vehicle record	219
Vehicle Schedule of Field Trips	220
Mileage Log	220
Requisition for parts of vehicles	221
Vehicle Master Maintenance Schedule	222
Vehicle maintenance record	223
Vehicle repair log	223
CHAPTER SEVEN:	224
Non-profit / NGO warehouse management:	224
Defining warehousing:	224
Warehouse Management Diagram No 42:	225
Warehouse ledger:	226
Warehouse Inward Register:	227
Warehouse Outward Register:	228
Warehouse Inventory:	229
Warehouse Receiving and Issuance Log:	230
Supply inward record:	230
Weekly Warehouse Report:	231
StockInventory:	232
Vehicles Spare Parts Stock Inventory:	233
Shipping Note Book warehouse:	234
Warehouse Receiving and issuance Log Format 2:	235
Warehouse Bin Card (discrepancy):	235
Warehouse Bin Card (discrepancy) :	236

Shipping Invoice:	237
Order acceptance Notice	238
Waybill	239
Claim for Shipment damage	240
Consignment Delivery Not	241
Confirmation of goods (Materials) Receive	242
Shuttle - Driver trip log:--	243
Release ord	243
Stock Count:	244
Expected Shipments	245
CHAPTER EIGHT	**246**
Non-profit / NGO's Human Resources Management:	246
NGOs'Human Resources Management:-	246
Definition HRM:	246
HRM Diagram No 4	247
NGO Human Resources Management:	247
Manpower request	247
Job Description Fo	250
Job advertisement:	251
Interview form:	252
Interview Form Page 2:	253
Rejection	254
Acknowledgment of Application	255
An offer of Employment Letter	256
Offer Letter	257
Joining report	258
Employees'Profile (Excel Sheet)	259
Welcome New Employee Letter	260

Employee Orientation Manual	261
Employee Fact Sheet	262
Reference checking form	263
Previous job checking form	264
Probation evaluation:	265
Probation extension letter:	268
Employment letter after probation:	269
Promotion Letter:	270
Employee benefit survey:	270
Employee Performance Review:	272
Employee self-evaluation:	273
Increment Letter	274
Office Circular Note	275
Employee status form	276
Employee Status Report:	277
Payslip letter:	278
Disciplinary Steps: -	279
Training Need Assessment:	280
Written reprimand:	281
Disciplinary Action Record	282
Final Warning Letter:	283
Verbal Warning Letter	284
Verbal Warning Letter:	284
Notice of unsatisfactory Performance	285
Show Cause Letter:	286
Suspension Letter;	287
Relieving Letter:	288
Receipt of Written Reprimand	289
Resignation Accepted:	290
Termination Letter:-	291
Termination Notice:	292

CHAPTER NINE:	293
Types of Reports:	293
Narrative Reports:	294
Financial Reports:	294
Tips on Writing Effective Progress Reports:	297
The SMART	297
Plan of Operation	298
Daily Progress Report	299
Site Visit Report	300
Site visit report page 2	301
Site visit report page 3	302
Daily Progress Report	303
Daily Progress Report	303
Project lessons learn report	304
Project Narrative Report	305
Project Narrative Report page 2	305
Budget Monitoring Report	306
Change of Assignment Log	307
Issues/incident Log	307
Activities Scheduling Log	308
Resource Scheduling	309
Field Staff risk/issues identification Log	309
Field Staff Monthly Report	310
Field Staff Monthly Report	311
Action Planning Log	312
CHAPTER TEN	313
Project proposal writing techniques	313
Project Proposal main points	314
See Diagram No 45:	314
Bibliography and References:	316

Preface

The purpose of this book is to bring to managers and field staffs of NGOs hands-on tools and standardized procedures that ensure viable systematic documentation, without which NGOs would not be able to earn credibility and integrity for internal and external monitoring. The book contains practical tools and procedures for beginners, mid-level and senior NGOs staffs that ensure proper understanding of modern-day systematic documentation of NGOs operation. It aims to bring about operational Standard Operating Procedures to systematically document progress on projects.

Generally speaking, there are many books you will find on NGOs management, but the current book that you have in your hands is different in the sense that it emphasizes practical over theory. The book calls for a system to be in the place that ensures credibility and integrity on the part of NGOs. Smart documentary evidence by following SOPs ensures NGOs' internal and external accountability. As for example, administrative SOPs ensure smooth functioning of NGOs' staffs by bringing forward policy tools for facilitation and healthy working environment. Financial accountability can be brought forward by following finance SOPs. NGOs can earn approval and credibility of donors by following certain practical procedures and also can ensure internal accountability and proper and smooth functioning of an organization's hierarchy.

NGOs are formed and perished, why? It is because they do not follow proper procedures, no matter how the knowledge you have, but it is the practical documentation of your project operation that counts. Unless and until you know these practical procedures and applying them, you never get to the donors or foster that relationship. So no NGO can compromise its practical viability by having no practical procedures to follow. Donors' approval comes with practical viability and that in turn comes with having to follow practical procedures that govern NGOs operation. So if there are no practical governing rules and procedures of an NGO, then there will be no donors to approve of your projects.

The book incorporates nearly all SOPs currently in practice pertaining to NGOs administration, human resources management, finance management, logistics and warehouse best practices, report writing, practical project management tools, practical community mobilization techniques and proposal writing. So the book caters to the needs of all NGOs staffs ranging from NGO kick Starter to field staffs, senior-level managers and board members. Many key concepts are being presented diagrammatically to make them understandable in a more lucid manner and put them to practice.

I acknowledge all those training institution, friends and colleagues that gave me food for thought which culminated in writing this practical book for all NGOs staffs.

Introduction

NGO and project management systems though seem to be two different separate systems governing today the world of NGOs, but in practice, the two are inter-dependent and inter-related terms used to describe a range of systematic practical steps to better manage the resources and funds that NGOs get to implement projects pertaining to people's environment(both physical and non-physical), behavioural change, capacity building, belief systems transformation that lead to the overall growth of individual or society/community development. Over the years, experts and organizations have developed practical systems and tools that govern NGOs and its projects to better manage resources and funds so that the troika (people, NGO and donors) are made responsible and accountable to each other.

If NGOs have funds for projects, then there is the need for a certain financial management system to book keep the inflow and outflow of funds. Different departmental standard operating procedures are developed to govern better the day to day affairs of NGOs to have a better congenial working environment both inside and outside of NGOs' operation.

This guide capitalizes on those practical SOPs regarding projects and NGOs' management that ensure proper departmental functioning of an organization and its project management. This guide is a practical guide in the sense that it describes all those practical project management tools, community mobilization practical techniques and standard operating procedures that govern the operation and policies aspects of an organization. Chapter one defines NGO, its history, evolution and registration process. Chapter two describes the concepts and practices round project cycle management. Chapter three elaborates community mobilization techniques and tools and sheds light on CMTs that evolved through the history and their current application in modern-day community mobilization. Chapter four consists of NGOs financial management concepts and SOPs currently in use to better manage NGO's finances. Chapter five capitalizes on administrative standard operating procedures which work towards better management between different departments to create congenial workforce environment. Chapter six and seven deal with logistics and warehouse standard practices and operating procedures. Chapter eight deals with human resources management standard operating procedures following which better workforce can be hired and put to work towards the realization of NGO's mission. Chapter nine describes different report formats that are required from an organization's staffs and also to meet the donor's requirements. Chapter ten is about the techniques to write grant proposals.

CHAPTER ONE

Defining an NGO:

NGO, basically a volunteer organization which strives to further the interest of those who lack basic amenities, services and humanitarian assistance in case of internal and external conflicts and in need of better environment (social, cultural, political non-aligned to a party or favouring one political party over another, economic, legal, technological, pollution-free physical environment), building people's capacity to be better citizens of a country. NGO strives to arrive at a better environment both physical and non-physical to keep it from degradation. NGO takes interest in advocating and furthering people interests as a catalyst to bring about social change by bringing attitudinal change in people through advocacy and lobbying and thereby influence socio-economic and political policymaking as non-aligned, not favouring one party over another and not influenced by any party or government, but as the catalyst. NGOs strive to put people on the track of struggle to master their own destiny and keeping their dependency syndrome to a minimum and thereby making them be informed citizens of a country and thus bringing about change in their environment both socio-economic and political and physical, cultural, legal and technological advancement. So environment, behaviour change, capacity building, attitudinal change and social change are the main thematic areas of NGO intervention.

So I can define NGO as a volunteer organization not- for- profit, non-political that strives to bring about change in people environment (both physical and non-physical), behaviour, capacity and attitude and thereby making them tie to the social fabric as a unit and contributing to bring about social change.

The Operational Directive 14.70 of the World Bank defines NGOs as: "private organizations that pursue activities to relieve suffering, promote the interests of the poor, protect the environment, provide basic social services, or undertake community development" (World Bank 2001). **[1]**. According to the World Bank, NGOs are "value-based organizations which depend, in whole or in part, on charitable donations and voluntary service," and in which "principles of altruism and voluntarism remain key defining characteristics". So here the World Bank gives two main characteristics to the word NGO, which are, altruism (giving one's own to others even if you need it, or giving one own where you deem fit its need) and volunteerism (giving one's own more than your needs)

Schmidt and Take define NGOs as thus "Non-governmental organizations (NGOs) are generally considered to be "non-state, non-profit orientated groups who pursue purposes of public interest", excluding the private sector (Schmidt and Take 1997) **[2]**. So Schmidt and Take definition is inclusive of those organizations which are not state influenced and not mandated for-profit and they exclude those private sectors that can be either partisan, non-partisan but exclusively stand for profit.

Category of NGOs:

There are two main categories of NGOs:

Mutual Benefit NGO:

This category includes those NGOs which come into existence to further and defend the interests of its members, as a trade union, youth clubs, associations, as sports association, teacher association, student association, etc.

Public Benefit NGOs:

The category of NGOs is public-oriented and include those NGOs which stand for furthering and promoting public interests at the expense of individuals and strive to serve the society as a whole and struggle to tie up individuals to their social fabric by incorporating their needs into a whole of society and not just individuals. So here the social fabric is kept intact by serving individuals without any narrow interests of individuals or any marginalization based on narrow interests of a few. So a public benefit NGO is non-discriminatory, non- partisan, not narrow in its interests, public-oriented, keeping the social fabric intact, not for profit, outside of government influence, furthering and promoting public interests.

Types of NGOs

The World Bank describes two types of NGOs based on their interaction and their role-play:

Operational NGOs:

These NGOs are concerned with the implementation of developmental projects having their donors and its full-fledged headquarter where they and their donor agree upon a plan of operation to launch a developmental project for the interest of the public at large or segment of the marginalized community. So the main principles of these NGOs are that they have full-fledged headquarters (international or national) with full or part-time employees and operational plan based on their project proposals and implementation strategies, providing services, building the capacity of the target people resulting intangible benefits to the people.

Advocacy NGOs:

The main purpose of these NGOs are to further or promote a cause of concern and catch public attention to that cause/issue that is going to worsen or make right the situations. Usually, they do this through public gathering, mass awareness, mass campaign through media, and seminars arrangement on an issue of public concern or cause, holding peaceful demonstrations and peaceful public rallies for bringing change in attitude and public policies, internationally or nationally.

Characteristics of NGO:

No bureaucratic hierarchy and functionality:

NGOs are not bureaucratic in their function as government line departments are governed through a bureaucratic hierarchy based on competition, codes and the attitude attached with it. On the other side, NGOs are largely interactive in their functionality and believe in intra and interpersonal relationships and are not governed by bureaucratic codes of behaviour.

Altruism

NGOs are altruistic in nature doing things out of public spirit and service. Government bureaucracy is distracted by codes of behaviour and conduct from social welfare, and private business concerns are profit prone and pay little attention to sectors that require altruistic welfare active involvement as NGOs are always up to perform public welfare activities. (Example: What happens when a bureaucrat and a social worker see a person jumps or slips into deep water in their presence? The bureaucrat will respond by gathering information and falling into procedural methods to take the person out of the trouble. But a social worker jumps to the water straight away to take the person out of the water by risking his own life.

Volunteerism:

Volunteerism is the core value/ characteristic of NGOs. Peoples give their money, time, resources (tangible or intangible) to a particular cause, the movement that they consider most valuable in terms of serving a segment of society or the society at large. For example, Angelina Jolie (Hollywood Actress) associated herself voluntarily with UNHCR to serve, collect and contribute to the cause of refugees' crises all over the world. NGOs board of trustees and executive body is also serve as volunteers towards a cause and for the implementation of a project, though there are certain project-based employees or some permanent employees at their headquarters to look after NGOs matters.

work towards raising the standard of living:

Every NGO strives towards the betterment and escalating standard of living for a specific segment of society or the society at large to achieve certain goal/purpose to bring improvement in the standard of living for the target people through the implementation of a project that sector-specific and having a certain specific purpose.

Tying up people with line departments

As per civil society, peoples are governed by certain laws, rule and regulations, but most often this bureaucratic power dynamic widens up the gap between people and line government departments. This power dynamic is broken up by NGOs' interventions by building peoples' trust and confidence to get what is due to them.

Classification of NGOs:

NGOs are further classified into:

INGO:

International organization having its headquarters in a country other than the country in which it operates or advocates. These are organizations with broad operational or advocacy plans having headquarters, permanent employees, project-based full time or part-time employees and registered with a registering government authority based on the laws of that country in which it operates., as for example, Save the Children, Oxfam. Some of these INGOs are backed up or funded by developed countries public money to help people of that country in which that INGO operates. So a major chunk of public money in the form of donation is spent through the help of those foreign government-backed up INGOs, as, Canada (CIDA), Switzerland (Swiss Agency for Development and Co-operation (SADC) (SIDA). United States of America (USAID), Great Britain (DFID), Japan (JICA), Germany (GTZ) etc. These INGOs also gives funds to national NGO to help implement projects in that country.

These INGOs are not mandated or backed up by international laws except ICRC (International Committee of the Red Cross, founded in 1863) since it is based on Geneva Convention. [3]. So ICRC cannot be classified as INGO. ICRC is an exception as it is neither a United Nations Organization Agency like UNDP nor INGO as USAID and DFID.

National NGOs:

This class of NGOs is registered entities with government registering authority but outside of government influence according to the laws of the land within the geographical boundaries of a country in which it operates. National NGOs have their headquarters in the country in which it operates. National NGOs depend largely on donors, INGOs and UN agencies to implement projects within the geographical boundaries of that country. They have their own bylaws and ruled and abide by them.

CBOs (Community Based Organizations:

These organizations are limited to region within the geographical boundaries of a country and are not mandated or backed up by law to operate within the whole of the country or covering all regions of a country like national NGOs. They can be operational or advocacy NGOs or both, but certainly will be having the mandate to serve a specific region or community within their resources, and mostly dependent financially on individual or INGOs to implement projects.

History and Evolution of NGOs:

History and Evolution of NGOs: The term which stands for Non-governmental Organizations is a known phenomenon in today's world and dates back to 2,500 BC. It is not known who coined this word NGO, but the term, "non-governmental organization" or NGO, came into use in 1945 because of the need for the UN to differentiate in its Charter between participation rights for intergovernmental specialized agencies and those for international private organizations". Ali Mostashari, an introduction to non-governmental organization management, 2005[4] Today different names have been given to these organizations depending on the scope, roles, functions that they perform. Sometimes they are called "civil society organizations (CSOs)", "non- profit organizations (NPO)". International Committee of the Red Cross is the oldest organization so far its scope and role is concerned and was founded in 1863. After the industrial revolution, a large pole of the international organization has been formed, but some of them survived and some disappeared during World War II. After World War II the NGOs sector flourished and many national and international NGOs were formed and their roots got deep into societies as they focused on humanitarian concerns, as service provider after the government of a country.

The importance of NGOs was officially recognized by the United Nations at the UN Congress in San Francisco in 1968, a provision was made in Article 71 of the Charter of the United Nations framework that let the NGOs have their consultative say in the field of economic and social development with the Economic and Social Council. Modern NGOs sector took its shape after World War II and a great deal of their care for humanity established their credibility in the masses.

Modern NGOs - historical perspectives

Modern NGOs evolved through history and they are now an established phenomenon in shaping policies and economic development and have a great deal of impact on world politics and economic development. The Modern Welfare States is an example of NGOs advocacy for the cause of humanity. They worked for the betterment of societies and advocated and implemented projects that promoted human rights, access to education, human capital capacity building, better environment, democracy, freedom, technological advancement, bringing about attitudinal change that shaped societies and nations for social change to take place. Abolition of slavery and bonded labour, workers' welfare, free primary education and access to education, social welfare, respect for human rights, women education and streamlining into politics, freedom of expression, political asylum and many instances of modern-day movements were backed and supported by NGOs.

Postmodern NGOs are now more concern bringing about social change by incorporating primary stockholders' opinions into their operational plans through a consultative process that result in tangible benefits to them and thereby making them master their own destiny leaving NGO to play the role as an expert catalyst.

So old NGO thematic area was only humanitarian assistance, modern NGOs took off as movement and policy change have driven and postmodern NGOs are now more concern to influence policies of governments through strong lobbying and campaign and to implement projects through a consultative process with primary stockholders and thus making people master their own destiny and leaving to NGOs the role to play as catalyst. So many concepts and practices introduced into postmodern NGOs conceptual and operational plans for implementing projects to make them more accountable to people and donors.

The role of NGOs in community development:

Let's examine and define the words "community" and "development"

Community:

Community is a social body of individuals having some specific geographical boundaries, common culture, common language, common mental and physical orientation, and common socio-economic, political conditions.

Development

From NGOs perspective, development can be taken in the meaning of transforming community environment, socio-political conditions, building capacity for change in behaviour and belief system and setting some definite goals to achieve with the active participation of the community.

Community development:

t's a process where government efforts are supplemented or corrected by NGOs with peoples' active participation to improve their socio-economic, political, environmental, legal, technological and cultural environment that affects their livelihood conditions. So community development is a holistic process of bringing change into peoples' environment, behaviour, capacity, belief system and overall mission and goal they set to achieve through their active participation.

See Diagram No 1 below.

Diagram No1 (Community Development):

The role of NGOs in community development:

What NGOs perform regarding community development? Potentially the main work of NGOs is to fill those gaps, supplement or at least strike a balance out of altruistic spirit where governments or the community itself cannot reach to or create conditions to realize its true potentials. In modern days, NGOs are now concern more with the democratic values to get people on board, put them to analyze their socio-economic conditions, political policies and decision effecting their livelihood conditions for the realization of their true potentials, changing their belief/value system regarding conditions to bring about change in their behaviour and attitude towards their overall development and removing dependency syndrome upon government bureaucracy and to stand on their own.

NGOs in the current development scenario do not stand for hurried herding peoples toward their problem solving or getting them to try new ventures without their participation, but NGOs are change agents in the sense that on one hand, they bring about a social change and on other hands they use this social change to make people realize their true potential by ensuring their greater participation with regard to their socio-economic, political, environmental, cultural, technological and legal systems.

NGOs are not parallel to governments in their working conditions, but at times add to government efforts to bring about an overall change in individual life and collective lives. NGOs develop local resources and means that the community own by their active participation. As Julius Nyerere in 1968 [5] said, "Rural development is the participation of people in a mutual learning experience involving themselves, their local resources, external change agents, and outsideresources .People cannot be developed. They can only develop themselves by participating in activities which affect their well-being. People are not being developed when they are herded like animals into new ventures." The developmental process is not hurried herding peoples towards trying new ventures, but it's a process to ensure peoples' greater participation towards realizing their true potentials.

Diagram No 2(understanding community development):

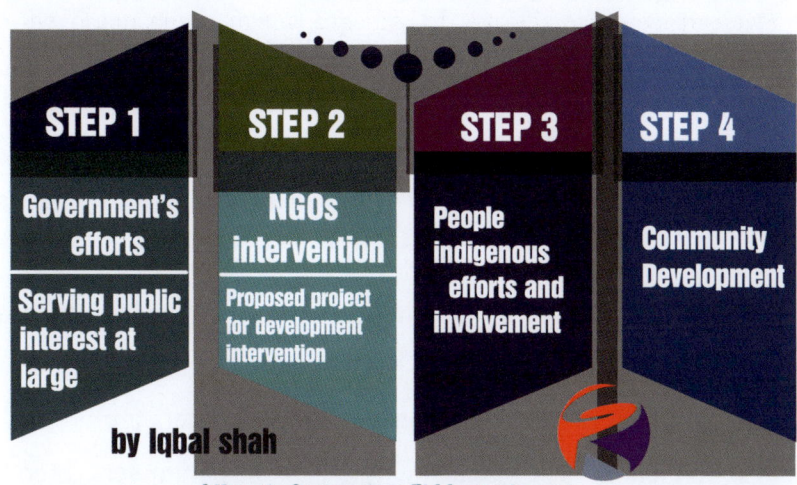

Registering an NGO:

Every country of the world has its own regulatory authority regarding NGOs' registration. So, first of all, you have to know which authority or body, department or ministry of government you have to register with.

Development of Vision and Mission statements:

Vision statement is that the overall goal of an organization that it stands for. For example, "Together we stand for humanitarian assistance, eradicating poverty, mass awareness for human's rights". A mission statement is what the organization wants to accomplish. For example, "Creating and having a world free of discrimination, educated, healthy, and skilled and thereby facilitating and helping peoples master their own destiny".

Developing aims and objectives

The board members and executive body are responsible to develop aims and objectives for the organization that the organization will accomplish in the near future. Aims and objectives are based on a sectoral level, as mass human right advocacy, formal and non-formal education, health hygiene, etc.

NGOs Bylaws Development

NGO bylaws are those regulatory statutes or laws that are made through consensus by the Board of Director and Executive Body before registering it through which its functions, aims and objectives, roles and duties of officeholders are defined. Amendments in bylaws are also defined in these statutes within a set of parameters. It consists of NGO's official name, its type, aims and objectives, membership criteria and qualification, executive and general body formation, office bearers' functions, duties, roles and responsibilities, governing structure and future plans.

Board of Directors:

A new phenomenon has evolved regarding the structure of NGO after postmodernism to have a Board of Directors consisting of people with specialized interests and expertise to better regulate the functions of it through constant surveillance measures thereby making an NGO more responsible and accountable to primary and secondary stockholders. So it is an administrative and consultative body in its nature constantly overseeing NGO administrative and financial matters, discuss policy matters and devising strategies regarding its projects and operational plans. The board appoints chairpersons for a specific time who steer the course of action through consultation with other board members.

Executive Body:

NGO executive body consists of that seven or nine-member team who are permanent members of the NGO who play their roles and take responsibilities as enjoined in the NGO bylaws. The body is either permanent or change roles and responsibilities as defined in the bylaws of the NGO. The body is responsible and accountable to the board of directors through its chairman or president, what that name may be, and who is appointed by the executive body and board of directors to direct the course of actions as advised by the body and board.

General Body:

NGO may also have a body of general members who either associate themselves with it by their interests or who see or give whatever their valuables in terms of fulfilling its aims and objectives. The NGO match their interests either by serving their interests or the society at large, therefore they join it out of a purpose.

Function, duties, roles, and responsibilities of NGO members:

As mentioned above, the roles, duties, functions and responsibilities are set forth in the NGO bylaws of its Board of Directors, Executive and General Bodies within certain set parameters.

CHAPTER TWO

Project Cycle Management (PCM)

Let's examine these three words at the start, that are, Project, Cycle and Management

What is a project or what is meant by a project through NGO perspective?

A project is intervention logic in community unfavourable socio-economic, political, environmental, social, cultural, legal, technological, behaviour and attitude situations to arrive at favourable situations regarding attitudinal and behavioural change and humanitarian concerns through concerted efforts and plan of actions and strategies by involving a segment of society or society at large, within a specific time limit, using the democratic value of for the people, of the people and by the people. The core characteristics of the project are that it is time-bound, involving primary stakeholders, cost bound, specific in only one purpose, meant for a certain specific community. A project is a strategic plan of actions performed by certain staff members by involving beneficiaries to achieve a specific purpose within a time frame and budget. United Nations Population Fund defines a project in "Capacity Building of NGOs in Post-Conflict Situations" [6] "A project is "a multi-task activity with a purpose, a clearly developed plan, a budget, and a team to implement it within a specific timeline." See diagram No 3.

Diagram No 3 (project definition):

Defining Project

In other words, a project is a set of activities with operational and advocacy plan aims at achieving certain valuable results or outputs for a target group of individuals, or society at large, time and cost bound and having specific tangible results which lead to a bigger goal at the end to achieve. Donors have their own set of thematic areas to be addressed through projects and the implementing partner (NGO) sees those thematic areas which match their own aims and objectives and thus tries to put forward a project proposal to donors on a set format given to them by donors to describe its course of actions and flow of strategies to achieve whatever donors want them to achieve relating to a sector and addressing a segment of population or the society at large.

Every donor has its own thematic areas or sectors to be addressed in its projects. Some may work on health issues or health sector, education, infrastructure development, human capacity building, certain specific skills learning, keeping physical environment from degradation, population welfare, and some other may work on human rights, child rights, women rights, labour rights, bonded labour, child labour eradication and certain specific segment of population rights; still others may work on larger scale sectors affecting the whole of society at large as narcotics control, poppy crop eradication, drug abuse and addiction, demining, refugees welfare, internally displaced people due to civil war or natural disasters.

It is for the NGO to see whether they have expertise in the sectors that the donors want them to address. So NGOs have to search for donors who match their own aims and objectives written in their constitution or bylaws. Donor tries to advertise widely their projects in print and on their own websites, and if an NGO matches donors criteria for funding they can ask for the proposal format to be filled in, and once they agreed on a set of parameters and criteria, the implementing partner submit a detailed project proposal for approval outlining budget, target population, objectives and goals to be achieved, operational and activities plans to be pursued to achieve the purpose mentioned in the project.

Project Cycle Management:

Project Cycle:

As mentioned in the project definition, a project is a set and flow of strategies to be implied and steps taken to arrive at better situations and fill those gaps of unfavourable situations that affect a segment of society or the society at large. See Diagram Numbers 4 and 5:

From problem state to the desired state of affairs

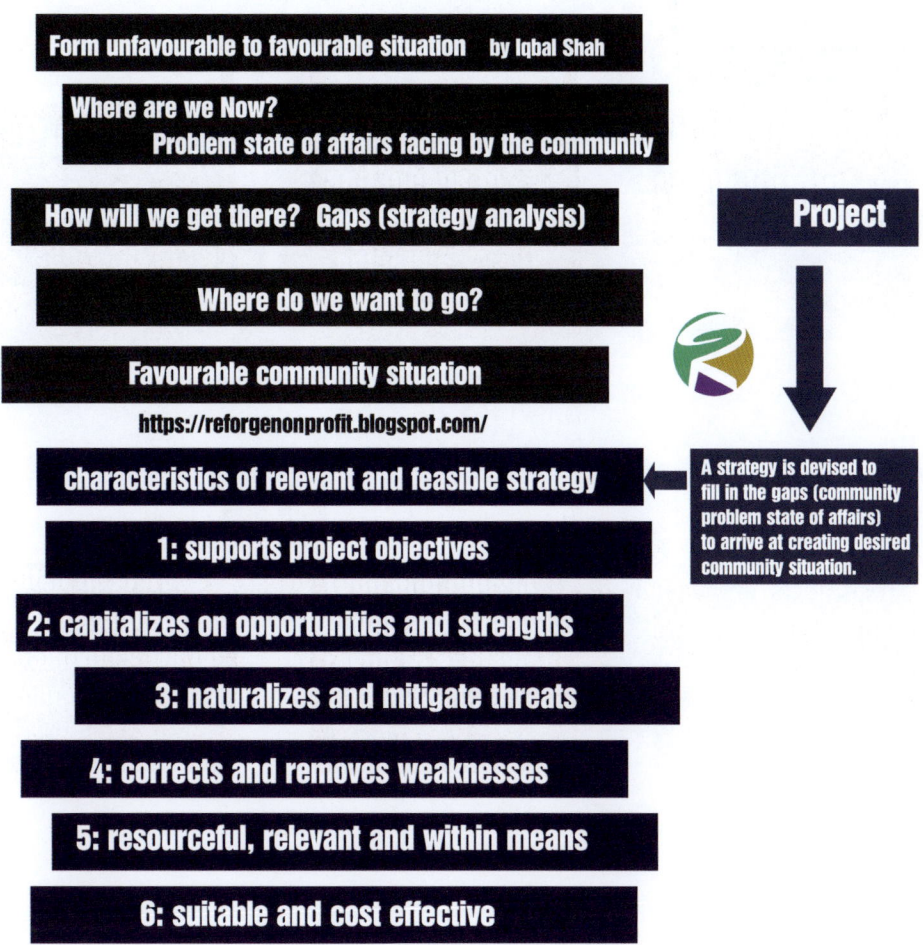

Diagram No 5:

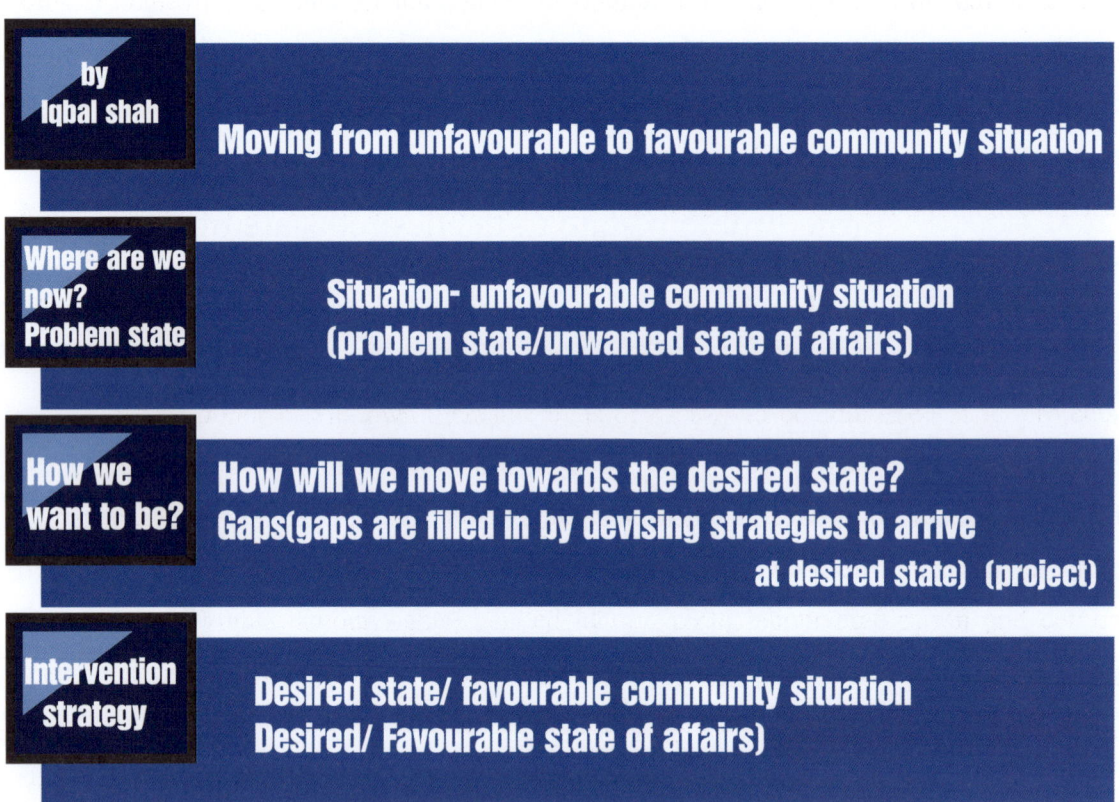

So projects are designed to adapt strategies or course of actions to move from unfavourable situation to favourable situations. A strategic course of actions that moves in a cycle in a systematic way to achieve a purpose in a community development context is called the project cycle.

Diagram No 6, Project Cycle Management:

Project Cycle Management

Identification → Appraisal → Financing → Implementation → Evaluation → Identification

Now, let's examine the three words (Project Cycle Management) together.

Project Cycle Management is a management style and strategic flow of work, plans, operational strategies through all stages of project cycle that have at its heart core logical framework, a tool to design and implement the operation plan of the project in a systematic way to achieve a specific purpose. See Diagrams Numbers 7, 8, 9, 10, 11, 12 and 13.

A Practical Guide to NGO and Project Management

Diagram No 7, PCM phases:

IDENTIFICATION	APPRAISAL	FINANCING	IMPLEMENTATION	EVALUATION
Idea Pick up	Idea futher development	Budget is prepared modalities are agreed upon	Resources and means are mobilized for project implementation.	Assessment of achievement by the project.
Sector Analysis	Consultation with beneficiaries		Project is executed	Lesson learned are shared and dissiminated.
Problem Identification	Problem analysis strategy analysis or objectives analysis	Formal finance agreement is signed between the donor and partner NGO to implement the project	Monitoring gets started and project reports are preapared	If the project is mid-term, then lessons are drawn up to further improve the project
Beneficiaries Involvement			planned versus actual progress is assessed. Changes and amendments are made in the operational plan according to changes in the circumstance	If evaluation is post-ante, then lessons and findings are shared for the purpose of improving the design of future projects.
Agreement on purpose and objectives	Feasibility study of the idea			
	Project sustainability study			
Relevance of the project idea is established	A formal project proposal is drawn up and presented to the donor for approval	BY IQBAL SHAH	Progress on objectives is regularly measured through indicators nad means of verification	Partner organization capacity is built up and experience through the project is further capitalized in future projects.

History of Log frame

In late 1960, logical Framework was first introduced by USAID to give a management style and meaning to its project. German GTZ gave it another name ZOOP, and all GTZ projects were managed through this. European countries adopted this management tool with the name ZOPP. And a full-fledged PCM which is at current at the core heart of every project was started using by European countries and it was JICA (JAPAN) which began the use of PCM as a full-fledged management tool for project management.

Characteristics of Project Cycle Management:

Change is constant, every time, and at any stage of PCM, change is the only constant.

Political, social. Cultural, ground realities (environment, both physical and non-physical) economic conditions, people's concerns and capacity to change behaviour and people attitude cannot remain the same. So you have to adapt strategies to go with the flow of change at every stage of PCM.

PCM is a project management tool that constantly needs adjustment, reviewing, change in strategies to mitigate risks and assumptions and to better manage the course of actions to arrive at objectives/ favourable situations intended.

Organizations are always in a constant learning process as the PCM itself, so with its change, organization growth and capacity to learn is inevitable.

Added to PCM is the Log Frame which is an operational plan management tool to develop plans and strategies, review and amend in accordance with changing circumstances to achieve a project purpose and thereby leading to a bigger goal.

PCM is a progressive management tool in the sense that each phase has to be completed for the next phase to be taken care of and tackled successfully.

As a management tool, PCM ensures that projects are relevant, purpose-oriented, sustainable in its long term goals and feasible in ensuring benefits to the target community, participatory in its design and implementation involving all stakeholders throughout the project circle, having provision for the projects' documents to be properly formatted, prepared and reported to bring transparency and accountability to the project. It ensures a smooth transformation from one phase to another.

LFA as describe in "project cycle management training handbook, May 1999 prepared by Information training and agricultural development ITAAD"**[7],** that project objectives are measurable in terms of quality, quantity and time against objectively verifiable indicators and thus provide basis for monitoring to take place to measure success or otherwise of the project by looking into OVIs and SOVs. Deviations at monitoring are properly taken care of so that the project adheres to its objectives to ensure achieving its purpose. So monitoring is a tool to learn lessons on the go and keeping the project on track and prevent deviations from project objectives.

Problem Identification Phase:

At this stage of PCM, problems of a community/ segment of society/ whole society or country are analyzed through the active involvement of primary stakeholders through surveys, questionnaire, focused group discussions, formal and informal interviews, site visits for rapport building by implying different techniques as drawing problem tree, problem web, rapid rural appraisal (RRA), participatory rural appraisal (PRA), experiential learning cycle(ELC), PIAPS(Problem Identification, Analysis, Priority Settings), for gauging target community problems by having that community on board through their active participation keeping in view their seasonal calendar and respecting their culture. This process requires and consumes more of your time as these are the primary sources of data collection in addition to background data collection as called secondary sources of data collection. The processes give the surveyors valuable insights into how they should proceed to identify problems and needs of the community as launching pad for the project.

So these processes give surveyors and project team insights into the needs of the target community to launch the project. It is careful consideration given to community problems and prioritizing those that need to be addressed and the community is willing to support. These surveys then can be used for short terms problems to be addressed through projects or can be used in future to launch big projects or cluster of projects for long term master plan development for community development.

All concepts of data collection, tools and community mobilization techniques will be discussed further in chapter 4.

Diagram No 8, PCM (Identification Phase):

Understanding PCM Diagrammatically

Project Cycle Management by Iqbal shah

- Identification
- Evaluation
- Appraisal
- Implementation
- Financing

https://reforgenonprofit.blogspot.com/

- Pre-project situation.
- Ideas development.
- Sector identification for intervention.
- Consultation with beneficiaries.
- Problems and needs assessment.
- Relevance of the project idea is established..

Appraisal Phase of PCM

At this phase of PCM, the idea of project intervention is further developed into operational project plan by involving all stakeholders through different techniques of community mobilization to give vent to people expression of opinion regarding that plan of intervention and study the feasibility and sustainability of that logic or idea of intervention more in detail. When the process of gathering primary and secondary data collection comes to its logical conclusion through stakeholders and objective analysis by implying different community mobilization technique, then a detailed project proposal is prepared by the management specialists to secure funding to intervene. The logic behind stakeholders and objectives analysis through community active participation is to avoid imposed decisions in regard to finding solutions to their problem and thus ensure greater sustainability of the project for longer terms. See diagram no 9:

Diagram No 9, from appraisal to proposal development:

From Appraisal to Project Development (process) By Iqbal shah

- Appraisal
- Moblizattion of community
- Stakeholders analysis
- Problem identification involving primary stakeholder
- Conducting survey using questionnaire, focused group discussion ,etc
- Drawing problem tree/web by involving primary stakeholders
- Problem analyis
- Objectives analysis
- Project proposal

https://reforgenonprofit.blogspot.com/

Diagram No 10, PCM (Appraisal phase):

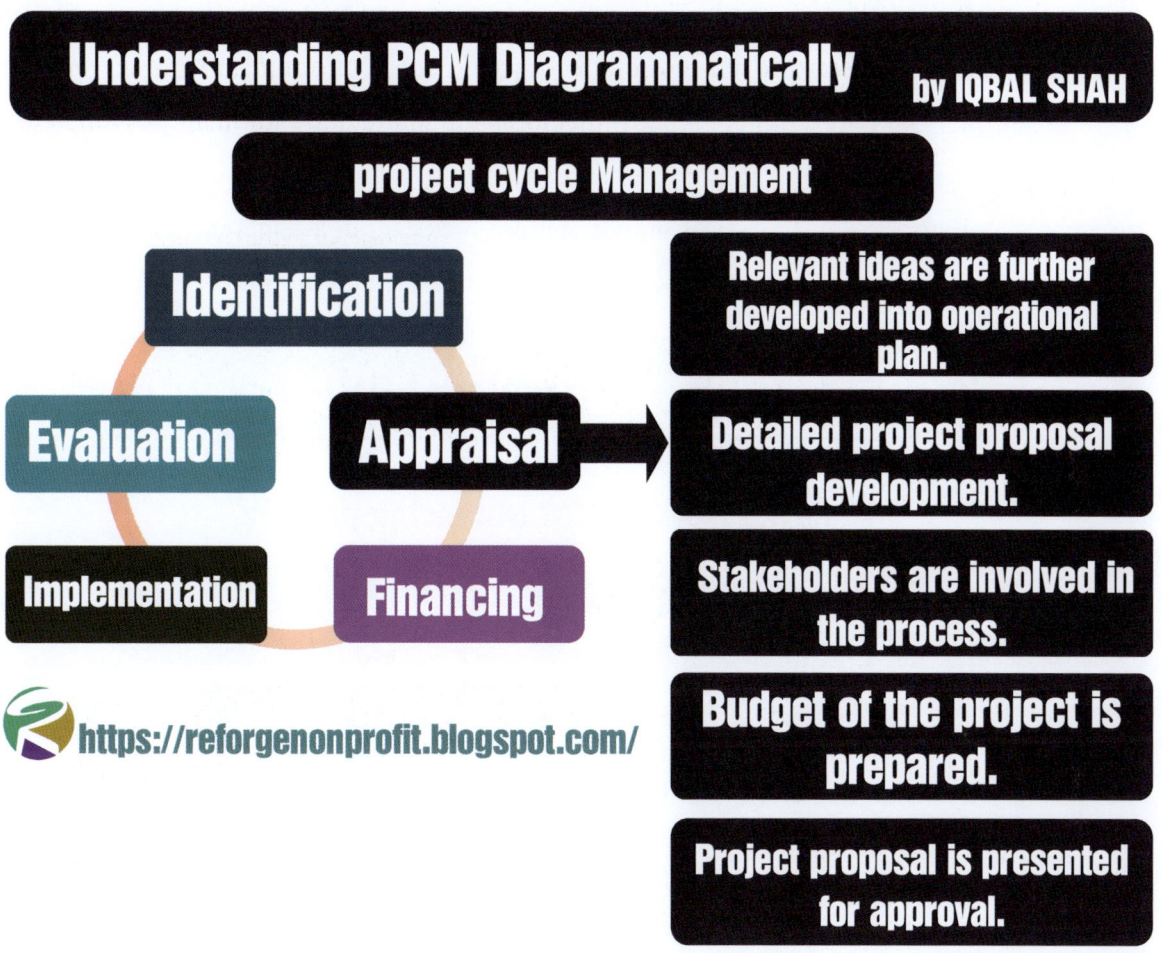

Project financing Phase:

Once the project proposal is developed, and the donor and the implementing NGO agree on TORs of financing and project, then the itemized budget is prepared to start working on the project. Means and cost are prepared; strategies formulated at the appraisal stage are further break up into coherent project design and operational plan to launch the project. Inputs and cost are examined and agreed upon to plan activities to achieve project objectives and purpose. Activities of the project are break up in a coherent way according to the agreed budget plan between the donor and its implementing partner NGO. So the financing TORs are developed and funding agreement is reached between the donor and NGO to implement the project. The funding agreement is a legal document between the donor and NGO and parameters are set for both the donor and NGO to implement the project within it.

Diagram No 11, PCM (financing phase):

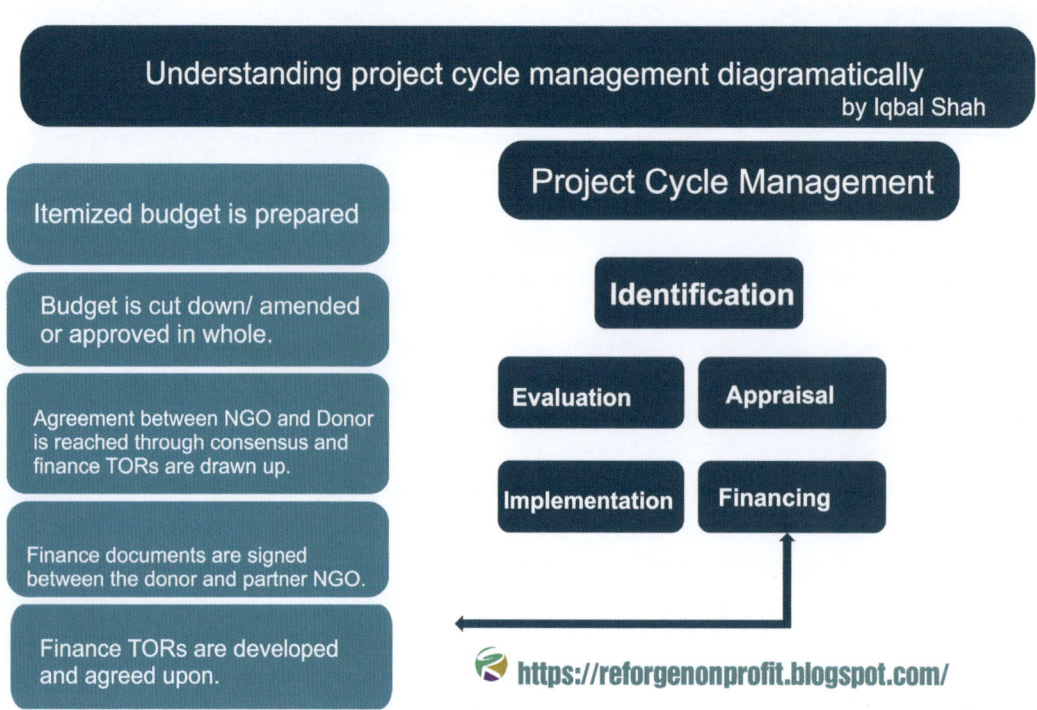

Project Implementation and Monitoring Phase:

During the implementation phase, project activities are launched, and project modalities are constantly going through the process of amendments and new inputs in term of technical knowledge, resource mobilization keeping in view the ground realities of project sector, assumptions, risks, stakeholders' consultation. The planned and actual activities are examined against the project objective and process monitoring takes place to amend, review and add new resources, technical knowledge to the project operational plan. So change is constant here at this stage and if necessary, some new dimensions and project objectives are added to it to keep the project on track in the light of new circumstances that emerge during this stage of the project. So monitoring, reviewing of objectives, amendments to activities and objectives are analyzed according to the new circumstances that arise during this phase.

I will describe monitoring a tool for learning lessons on the go to keep the project adheres to its objectives and prevent deviations to meet project and achieve project purpose in the manner planned. Planned versus actual progress is measured through objectively verifiable indicator and sources of verification. Project reports are prepared, accounts are straightened up, SOPs are followed and budget monitoring reports are presented to the donor.

Diagram No 12, PCM implementation phase:

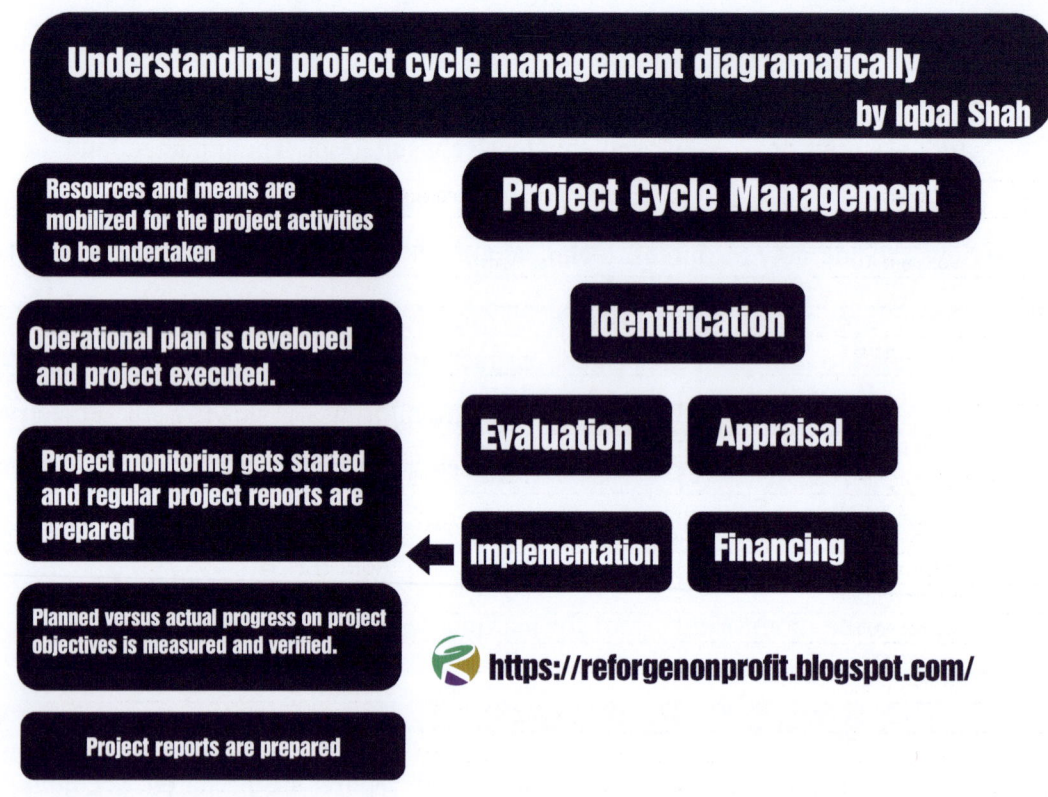

Project Evaluation Phase:

At this stage of the project, the donor and the implementing partner NGO assess the success of the project and information about it is exchanged and lessons learned are shared and thus these evaluation findings, lessons are further used future such type of project so that mistakes are not repeated and good practices are given due attention and diligence in the future or during the project.

Types of evaluation:

Mid-term Evaluation:

This type of evaluation is carried during the project to find loopholes and success points and apply the lessons learned to the remaining project duration. Donors and partner NGO usually carry mid-term evaluation to know if there are any shortcomings to remove and keep the project objectives on track and thus making the remaining duration of the project as successful as intended to bring tangible benefits to beneficiaries. The approach is participatory in nature involving all stakeholders or some of them.

Post-ante Evaluation:

When the main part of the NGO project reached its logical end, then post-project evaluation is carried out to know whether the project brought the intended benefits to beneficiaries. Findings are drawn and lessons learned are exchanged and shared and project success and closure report are prepared for further capitalization on them in the future projects. So lessons learned are further capitalized on in future projects.

Diagram No 13, PCM, phase evaluation:

Understanding Project Cycle Management — by Iqbal Shah

Project Cycle Management

- Identification
- Appraisal
- Financing
- Implementation
- Evaluation

Progress reports are prepared on regular basis to check and measure planned versus actual progress on project objectives

Mid-term evaluation is undertaken to find gaps in the project design and lessons learned are further applied to the remaining project as corrective measures.

Partner NGO and donors share what has been achieved at the end of the project by conducting post-ante evaluation.

Project closure report is prepared and lessons and findings are shared for improving the design of future projects. NGOs capacity is improved for further such type of project in the future.

https://reforgenonprofit.blogspot.com/

Main Characteristics of PCM

Every cycle stage is independent in its own right, and one stage successful completion leads to other stage beginning.

The stages are coherent in the way that one's success and failure lead to the success and failure of others.

PCM is a good planning tool that strives to achieve some specific purpose designed and intended.

A good planning tool that involves all the stakeholders and provides a platform to vent their concerns and address them according to their livelihood conditions, socio-economic, political, environmental, legal, technological and cultural perspectives.

It has the rooms for constant changes at every stage of it according to the new developments that arise during its phases. So what is constant is change and leaving rooms for change and improvements.

It has standard operating tools and techniques that minimize the chances of bad decisions and emphasizes quality and is focused on primary stakeholders' demand and project sustainability.

It emphasizes the better planning tools to arrive at better decisions in regard to the real needs of the beneficiaries.

Project documents are structured according to the standardized formats addressing all phases, assumptions and risks.

PCM is managed through a project management tool called Log Frame. Log frame is a management tool which is at the core of PCM to manage, reports project operational plan on project structured formats, identifies loophole and devising strategies to address them, and provide for process monitoring and evaluation of the project and draws lessons at the end of the project. In the following discussion, I would like to describe in details what this Logical Framework as design and implantation tool of project is?

Definition of Logical Framework:

Logical Framework is considered by nearly all donors and their implementing partners as a management tools that is being implied to design, sustain, review and amend the project implementation strategies and work plans in a logical systematic way according to the stages of PCM as they deem fit to reach and achieve project objectives and overall goal set forth in the project. The only constant in PCM and its logical Framework is changing.

See Diagram No 14 for Logical Framework Matrix

Characteristics of the Logical Framework:

Logical Framework is a management, design and implementation tool applied to stages of PCM to achieve the project goal.

The steps in it are coherent and logical which proceed in logical manners.

It is flexible and always in need of changes to it according to the work and operational plan.

It provides for the project different levels of objectives' relationship.

It sets indicators to check whether or not project objectives have been achieved or going to be achieved and the operational plans are to be amended and adjustment is to be made to achieve the project goal.

It is a tool to measure the project objectives against indicators to know that whether or not these objectives achieved.

It establishes a coherent logical relationship between inputs and outputs of the project.

It provides formats for the project to be reported.

A measurement tool to check progress on planned versus actual progress on project objectives.

Reporting cycle moves in cyclical manners from down to the top, that is, field staffs report to senior NGO's management and management prepare reports for donors.

It emphasizes that social change is linear and project objectives can be predicted in advance.

Logical Framework Analysis

The logic of LFA (Process) and LFM (Product) is that it starts from bottom activities, means (humans and otherwise) and cost (finance, budget) to top as reaching and achieving project overall goal. If inputs and means are gathered and given, then activities are undertaken to achieve results. The project purpose is delivered if results are achieved. There should be only one project purpose. The purpose achieved contributes to the over the goal of the project. See the Difference between LFA and LFM in Diagram No 15.

Difference between log frame analysis and matrix

Diagram No 15, the difference between log frame analysis and matrix:

Difference between log frame analysis and log frame matrix — By Iqbal Shah

- Log frame analysis explained as process
- involving stakeholders analysis
- problems identification and analysis
- Objectives analysis. Establishing cause and effect relationship and turning the same into means and ends solutions
- proposing strategies to address problems
- Selecting strategy to serve a purpose

Log frame Matrix is explained as product of LFA

- It is 4 by 4 matrix consisting of 4 rows and 4 columns outlining LFA
- Goal, purpose, outcomes, results and actvities are presented in nutshell vertically.
- It describes the LFA in nutshell
- OVIs, SOVs and assumption for goal, purpose, and results and means, cost and risk for actvities are described horizontally

https://reforgenonprofit.blogspot.com/

Let's see and examine this logic(4×4 matrix, vertical rows 4×4 horizontal rows) one by one starting from pre-conditions to budget, means, activities, result (and its horizontal relationship with the above line), project purpose and its horizontal relationship with the above line) , overall purpose and its relationship with the above horizontal line).

Preconditions

These are the conditions without which a project cannot be started unless they are fulfilled. These are the condition if properly taken care of can contribute to the successful launching and thereby achieving its purpose.

Finance:

Budget or finance of the project is very important because without budget activities cannot be carried out and thus results and purpose remain unfulfilled.

Means:

Means are those tangible (human resources, finance,) and intangible (organization's capacity, technical ability, knowledge) assets, sometimes called inputs, which deliver activities and in turn contribute to achieve the result and thereby reach to the target (goal).

Activities:

These are a plan of actions and strategies to be adapted to deliver results. It is a summary of those actions plan that delivers the project's results.

Results:

Results are those tangible outputs when inputs are given; culminate in bringing change in community situations with tangible results.

Purpose:

Every project has a purpose to achieve, that can be for a segment of society or society at large. This purpose is achieved when inputs are given, and when inputs are given, actions are undertaken, when actions are undertaken, results are produced, when results are produced, project purpose is achieved and this purpose, in turn, contributes to the overall goal of the project.

Assumptions

These are factors outside of project control but can affect project implementation and long term sustainability. Avoid killer assumptions and take all stakeholders on board.

Pre-conditions:

These are conditions that must be met before the start of the project.

Log frame vertical hierarchy

Diagram No 16 below:

Diagram No 16, log frame vertical hierarchy:

How Log Frame's vertical and horizontal co-relations and impacts are established?

This diagram shows the vertical logic relationship with the horizontal logic that how different levels of vertical and horizontal logic co-related and how Log Frame is developed vertically and horizontally and the relationship of each column is established with another and the impacts upon the stockholders are measured and verified?

The stronger is the correlation between the vertical and horizontal logic, the better will be the results, purpose and overall goal. A handbook" Project Cycle Management handbook by European Commission, May 1999" [8], splits this management tools into further two phases:

Analysis Phase

During this phase the logical Framework is used to analyze community problems and doing need assessment to develop a vision and intervention logic to move from unfavourable and undesired situation to favourable and desired situations based on a set of Technique Development, Interviews, Focused Group Discussion) and analysis of problems (implying techniques as Problem Analysis (Problem Tree, Problem Web), Experiential Learning Cycle, Objective Analysis, Stakeholders' Analysis and Strategy Analysis of this phase follows in a separate chapter three of this book. At the objectives analysis phase, strategies are developed to address the primary problem keeping in view the relevance, resources, stakeholders 'physical and non-physical environment of strategies.

Diagrammatically the structure of moving from problem to the desired state is described in Diagram No17.

Diagram No17, from problem state to the desired state:

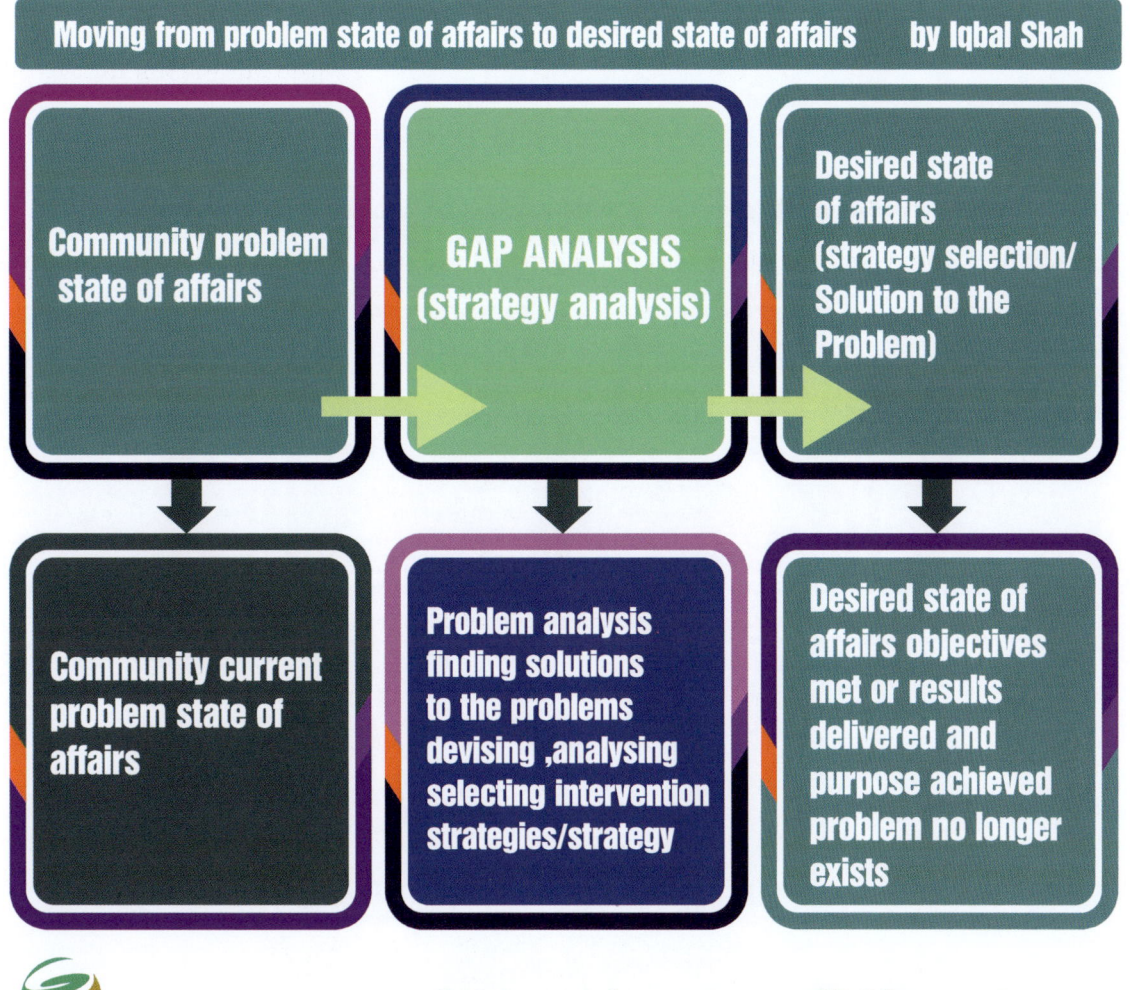

Planning Phase

This phase emphasizes the project ideas to be further developed into project's operational plan and strategies that were devised at the analysis phase and are put to test and that provide for a plan of action prepared to launch the project.

Diagrammatically the structure of the Planning Phase is described in Diagram No18.

Diagram No18, project planning phase

In the analysis phase of Logical Framework, different community mobilization techniques are implied to know and go into the depth and breadth of the real problems facing by beneficiaries/ primary stakeholders. The problem persists and can further create more complications and become more and more complex if not address at the right time with feasible strategies.

The work plan that is discussed in forum appropriate by involving all the stakeholders and thereby adapting cumulative approach starting from problem analysis (knowing the real needs of beneficiaries), objective analysis (what the project is going to bring to the beneficiaries in terms of benefits) and strategies analysis, that is, how to move the path of problematic situations to the desired community well off and better situations taking and keeping all stakeholders on track. Diagram No 19, from unfavourable to the favourable situation:

From Un-favourable to favourable situation

by Iqbal shah	Moving from unfavourable to favourable community situation
Where are we now? Problem state	Situation- unfavourable community situation (problem state/unwanted state of affairs)
How we want to be?	How will we move towards the desired state? Gaps(gaps are filled in by devising strategies to arrive at desired state) (project)
Intervention strategy	Desired state/ favourable community situation Desired/ Favourable state of affairs)

In this phase of analysis, strategies are put to test and thus the organization, primary stakeholders and the donors reached and agreed upon consensus strategies to be adapted for the project to be launched to address the primary issue/problem. The analysis of strategies on which the project operational plan is made is done through TOTE Model to move the way forward to achieve results and purpose of the project. So the gap between the problem state and the desired state of the community is filled in with strategies to be adapted to resolve community primary problem and all secondary and tertiary problem will be resolved by addressing the primary problem. So the best choice of strategies is made using TOTE Model as explained diagrammatically in diagram no 20.

Diagram No 20, TOTE Model for testing strategies:

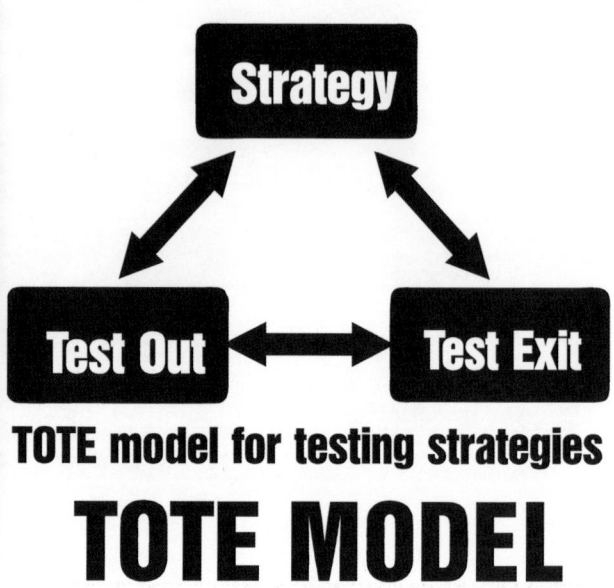

Community Mobilization Techniques

Community mobilization techniques are intended for those professionals who wish to enhance their knowledge and acquire the best skills needed for community mobilization around a cause. The book covers practical modern and conventional community mobilization techniques currently in use. The techniques aim to bring about a comprehensive strategic community intervention that minimizes the risk factors and capitalize on those factors that pave the way for a successful programme intervention aiming at community development or advocacy campaign.

The list of community mobilization is not exhaustive but comprehensive details have been added in order to make the readers grasp the subject matter well and apply the same to the situation intended for rapport building, community mobilization, community participation and organization.

This step by step guide book Teaches:

Practical insights to create community habits that stick

and constantly giving support, involvement and feedback

Actionable steps for rapport building needed for community mobilization and organization

Beahavioural and attitudinal techniques needed for habit-forming that support and inspire involvement

The diagrammatic presentation of the subject matter further adds to the lucid explanation of every community mobilization technique. The reader's interest in the subject matter has been taken care of as the graphics are presented well that make community mobilization techniques more easy to be grasped and applied.

Introduction to community mobilization techniques

Community mobilization techniques are a system in place that works towards community mobilization and organization. These tools and techniques aimed at bringing about change in people's environment (both physical and non-physical), behavioural change, capacity building, belief systems transformation that leads to the overall growth of individual or society/community development. Over the years, experts and organizations have developed practical techniques and tools that govern NGOs and its projects to better manage resources and funds so that the troika (people, NGO and donors) are made responsible and accountable to each other

Before going into discussing community mobilization, there are some terms which are sometimes confused and used interchangeably. Those experienced know the difference between community mobilizing and community organizing but those who are new to these concepts and their application will get to know that how these two terms are different and what if both concepts are used in the context of building trust and avoiding confrontation in the field.

People ask the question which one is first to be applied in the field? So here is the diagrammatic presentation that will clear the concepts/terms in a more lucid way that whether it is mobilization or organization that should come first? That is, which one is the process and which one is the product of that process? But going into that debate, let's discuss what social/community mobilization is? In the discussion of the following topic.

Community Mobilization(coneptual understanding)

I will explore what community mobilization actually is? What is the difference between mobilizing and organizing community? And what community development is?

Let's discuss what community mobilization is?

Before going to dig out more about the different social/community mobilization techniques, let's discuss first what social and community mobilization actually is? What is the difference between social mobilization and social organization, as community mobilizing and community organizing? What is social/community development actually is?

What community mobilization is?

Community Mobilizatio

Community mobilization is the process of involving, mobilizing and raising awareness level to the extent that the community feels free to express their concerns regarding their livelihood, socio-economic, political, environmental and cultural conditions that affect their lives and thereby making people find solutions to their problems in a sharing and caring environment they themselves create with minimal external control.

Participatory Process

Community mobilization ensures greater participation of primary stakeholders in the development interventions. For an evidence-based intervention and dispelling gender bias, primary stakeholders need to be involved in the decision-making process as the intervention logic means for them, as to remove conditions that impede their progress towards realizing their true potentials and also improving their living conditions so as to raise the standard of living. This participatory process inspires people indigenous knowledge and experience to invoke building consensus on mutual interests and benefits. The participatory approach to community development raises the level of community leadership and enhances their capacity to reach consensus to make decisions regarding community deprived life and livelihood conditions. The techniques are used to engage the community in the decision-making process. Local media as radio and TV platforms are used to build community capacity to engage in the dialogues to reach consensus on a solution to the problem that affects the community. Community members are empowered and engaged to identify, analyze the problems faced by the community. This community engagement results in capacity building of the community and later on culminates in invoking leadership acumen to reach consensus. The intended development intervention achieves its objectives once the beneficiaries/stakeholders participate in that very development process. The product (organized community) as a resultant of the process (community mobilization) leads to the achievement of the project overall goal.

NGO plays the role of a catalyst to restore and organize their energies around a cause, purpose or concern by implying different mobilization techniques. Participatory approach invokes transparency, accountability, ownership, sustainability.

Techniques with the community:

There are some rapport-building techniques that NGOs imply to come into good terms with the beneficiary/community at the start of building trust and later in community mobilization. A good community mobilizer must have the following qualities to establish rapport and building trust of the community in which he/she enters as a field supervisor.

1. For rapport and trust-building, a mobilizer must be warm-hearted to welcome and take people's question with concern.
2. He/she must be dressed in a proper way acceptable to that community, or at least must look like them.
3. A mobilizer must be culturally sensitive and should respect local tradition and religion.
4. Mobilizer must have the quality to take the most emotions provocative questions in manners appropriate and keep his/her cool.
5. A well-mannered mobilizer uses simple language to go into the depth of a specific community problem. He or she is soft-spoken and sympathetic in attitude.

Difference between community mobilization and organization

Community mobilizing and organizing:

Those experienced to know the difference between community mobilizing and community organizing but those who are new to these concepts and their application will get to know how these two terms are different and what if both concepts are used in the context of building trust and avoiding confrontation in the field. People ask a question which one is first to be applied in the field? So here is the diagrammatic presentation following that will clear the concepts/terms in a more lucid way that whether it is mobilization or organization that should come first? That is, which one is the process and which one is the product of that process?

In the process (mobilization) problems are presented, issues are brought forth, debates and discussion are held to know the root cause of the problem and to reach out to the primary problem first and then secondary and tertiary in order of preferences. It is a conflict stage that reveals people opinions, their indigenous knowledge, and heated discussion takes place to sort out the problem at hand. The process stage is a confrontational stage where the problem is analyzed and the consensus is built, and in the process, people differ in their opinion and solutions to the problem. So techniques are implied to reach consensus.

In the product stage, that is, community organization, the primary problem is identified and the consensus is built around a strategy to solve the primary problem and the project is ready to be launched. The planning stage of the project begins and the primary stakeholders are ready to give their best to make the project meet success.

Community mobilization is a process consists of the following:

Community mobilization phase:

It is issue-oriented, and mostly, the community is at the identification stage of the problem.

The community mobilization is driven by action that riddled the whole problem state of affairs

Stakeholder analysis is done at this stage of the problem state of affairs /project.

Problems are analyzed and they further categorized into primary, secondary and tertiary problems.

Objective analysis is done and solutions to the problems are presented.

Differences, heated discussions, debates mistrust permeate the whole community scenario.

Implying different mobilization tools and techniques to reach consensus

Community organization phase:

This stage of the problem identification is called the product stage of community mobilization phase.

At this phase, issues/problems are sorted and the community put solutions to the problems through consensus.

Differences of opinions are turned into a consensus.

Stakeholders trust is capitalized further to reach objective analysis.

Strategies to the problems are agreed upon.

Confrontation is turned into a consensus.

An action plan is developed to implement the project

Difference between community mobilization and organization:

Difference between community mobilizing and organizing by Iqbal Shah

Community mobilization is a process consists of the following	community organization is the product of community mobilization. (Product)...
Issue/ problem oriented	Issues/ problems are sorted out
Community Mobilization is driven by action	Time to take action and set objectives
Stakeholders analysis	Stakeholders trust has been built.
Problem analysis	Strategies to address the problem is agreed upon
Objectives analysis	Strategies to address the problem are reached out through consensus
Confrontation in nature as.............. ......different people ,different views	Confrontation is turned into consensus
Making to look for consensus by implying different techniques	Action plan is developed to implement the project

https://reforgenonprofit.blogspot.com/

Community mobilization is for community organization and when the community is organized, then comes the stage of participatory community development. So the community is mobilized and organized for its development and development experts play the role of catalyst and make all the stages of community development intervention participatory and engage the whole community in the development process so that the community feels ownership and accountability for what they do.

Community Development

Community Development — by Iqbal Shah

 https://reforgenonprofit.blogspot.com/

- Change in Environment (Both Physical and Non-Physical)
- Change in Collective and individual behaviour
- Change in capacity - by doing capacity building
- Change in Individual and collective Attitudes
- Change in People mission and goals (Ego change)
- Subsequent Resultant is community Development

What is community mobilization? Community: Community is a social body of individuals having some specific geographical boundaries, sharing some common traits and values, common culture, common language, common mental and physical orientation, and common socio-economic, political conditions. Development: From NGOs perspective, development can be taken in the meaning of transforming community environment, socio-political conditions and economic growth, building capacity for change in behaviour and belief system and setting some definite goals to achieve with the active participation of the community. Community development: is the process of committing a change in people overall collective environment, behaviours and attitudes and capacity building and bringing change in overall life conditions that hamper growth and impede the process of making informed choices and obstruct availing opportunities. Communities never work in a vacuum, but depend on each other to create opportunities and change livelihood conditions. So a fair and free environment is a prerequisite for a community to make informed choices and avail opportunities to strike a change in living conditions. Community development is a process where government efforts are supplemented or corrected by NGOs with peoples' active participation to improve their socio-economic, political, environmental, legal, technological and cultural environment that affects their livelihood conditions. Community development is a holistic process of bringing change into peoples' environment, behaviour, capacity, belief system and overall livelihood.

As for example, an NGO is actively involved in an advocacy programme to build consensus for the bill to be presented in the parliament pertaining to transgender rights and protection. It launches a series of advocacy mechanism (lectures, seminars, parliamentarian orientation programme, mass awareness through press releases and conference etc) to set the stage for a meaningful dialogue to happen and reach consensus through to make the law passed by the parliament. So in such circumstances, NGO supplements government efforts and strengthen its capacity to change a particular life condition that impedes the overall growth of a particular community.

In some cases, NGO corrects government policy decision regarding a particular life condition that hampers and impedes the livelihood condition, socio-economic growth of a particular community or group of people. In this case, NGO arranges rallies, press conferences, sign petitions, leads the peaceful procession and take some other steps necessary to compel the government to correct its policy decision regarding a particular life condition/situation.

Life conditions consist of people physical and non-physical environment, their capacity and skill to handle life situations, (as formal and non-formal education and skill learning), their behavioural and attitudinal change and appealing to their sentiments and intellect to bring change.

Government and NGO launch project to bring change in people livelihood conditions and remove circumstance and conditions that hamper people economic growth, capacity building and provide for living conditions that create fair opportunities for the community to avail to bring about change in their overall living conditions and livelihood conditions. So projects are launched to bring change in people overall physical and non-physical environment, behaviour, capacity and attitude. See the following diagram:

Community Development

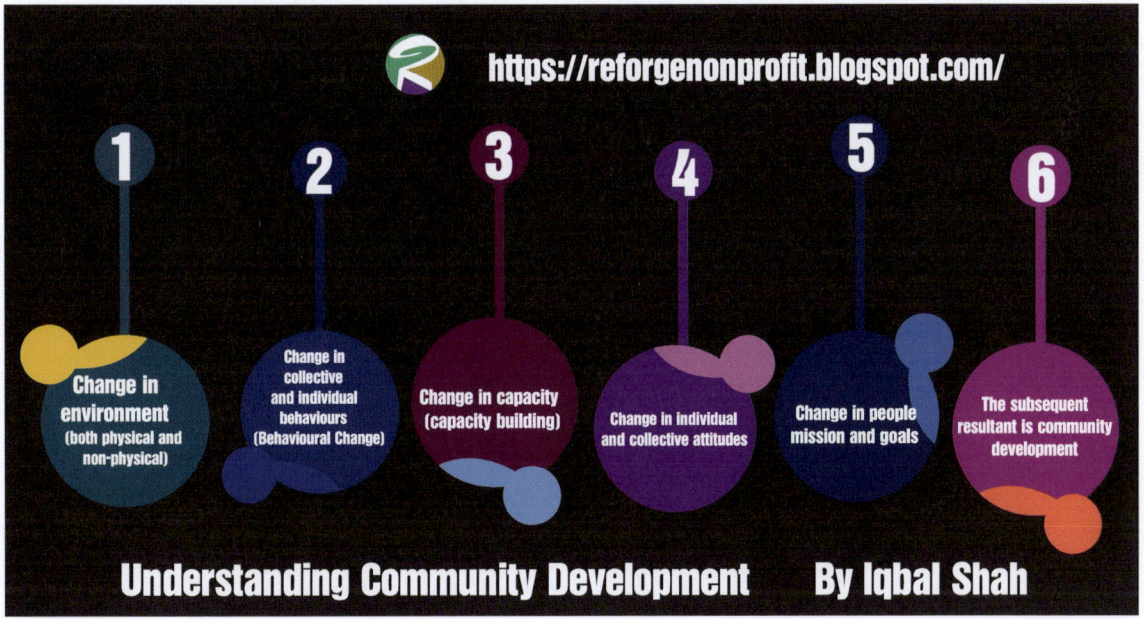

Projects bring people opportunities to avail so that they are able to change their circumstance, life and livelihood conditions in a free and fair environment grow economically and socially. Growth in the sense of economic development is possible when people avail opportunities and remove conditions that impede their livelihood conditions. Life conditions are changed when people are involved in the process of development and this type of development is called participatory development. People are involved from the inception of the development idea to the evaluation and summation of the development project. Participatory tools and techniques are applied to invoke people participation in the development project.

Understanding community development

Chapter 3

Participatory Approaches to Community Development:

Participatory Approaches:

In today's changing the world, developmental programmes and project are launched in a specific sector for a certain specific community in a time-bound manner with community active participation resulting in tangible and intangible benefits to them.

Target community involvement in different phases of the project:

The phenomenon to involve people in the inception process to project development and then onward from project to monitoring and evaluation of the project are done in such a way to involve all the stakeholders, especially the primary stakeholders in the development/advocacy process. The process of community development is incomplete with the active involvement of the primary stakeholders, as for which the intervention logic is developed. And not only the process of development such as identification of the problem, the inception of intervention logic, the planning phase of the project, implementation and monitoring and summation and evaluation of as end result/product of the process. So from process to product (project inception to project goal achievement), all phases of the project are made participatory as to make the target community let own the end results. With people, involvement project cannot be made sustainable, long-lasting. People involvement brings not transparency and accountability in the process, but also the target community feels ownership for long-lasting sustainable results/impacts/goal.

Sustainability factor and people' participation:

In this modern era of community development, intervening agencies are made bound by their donors to work for long-lasting sustainable impacts, so the intervening agency cannot ignore this sustainability factor as it makes the community own both failures and successes of the projects/programmes. Projects are owned by the community as they have involved from the very inception to evaluation phases of the intervention.

Different participatory techniques:

Different participatory techniques and tools are implied to ensure peoples' greater participation in these projects meant for them. Organizations play the role of catalyst and facilitators. Participatory approach invokes transparency, accountability, ownership, sustainability.

Community involvement:

Community participation is needed to ensure (1) people involved in the process of development; (2) and accountability on the part of an intervening agency, donors and primary stakeholders. Every intervention in the community living, working and livelihood conditions need to be participatory in nature, as this practice inspires support, involvement and feedback. Greater participation and involvement on the part of primary stakeholders can ensure due diligence. It also ensures accountability in humanitarian and development contexts and these further ads to the trust-building measures between the intervening agency and the primary stakeholders.

Participatory Learning and Action:

An umbrella term, "Participatory Learning and Action", is used for these mobilization and participatory techniques. These participatory tools and techniques aim at mobilizing the target community so as to ensure greater participation, leadership skills development. These tools and techniques also involve the marginalized, women and girls of the community, local leadership, indigenous community and youth. Some of good techniques and tools are Experiential Learning Cycle, Problem Identification Analysis Priority Setting (PIAPS), Participatory Rural Appraisal (PRA), Rapid Rural Appraisal (RRA), and Participatory Learning Method, Participatory Action Plan, Farming Systems Research, Baseline Survey, Interviews, Questionnaires, Focused Group Discussion. See the following diagram.

Diagram Mobilization /participatory tools and techniques

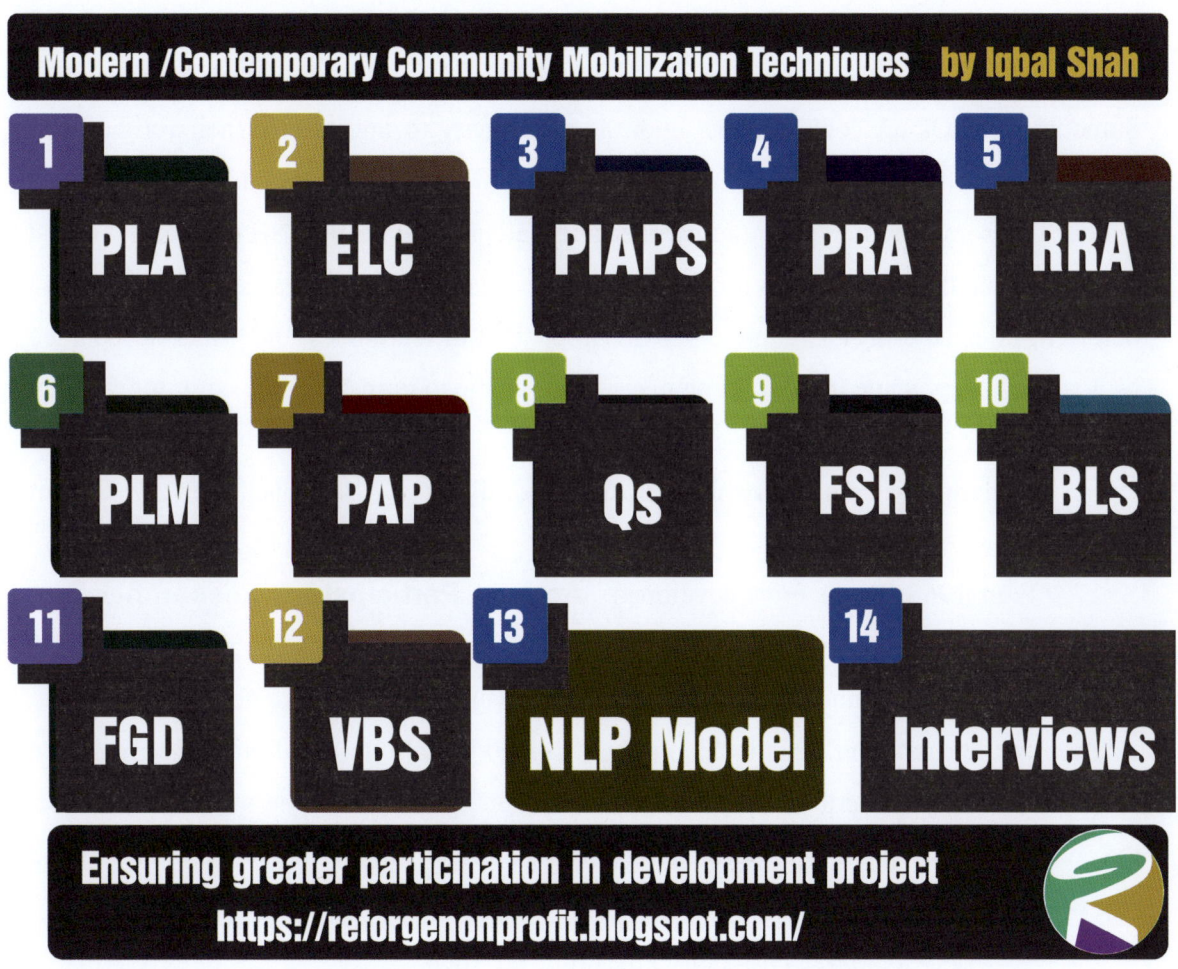

Modern-day challenges and community mobilization

Community mobilization in the modern day is a challenging task. It's not very easy to win over the people in order to gain their trust to accept NGO's intervention in a problem the community is facing. NGOs are termed sometimes as foreign agents working towards disrupting their cultural norms as perceived by a common man and woman. Sometimes NGOs are looked down upon as missionary to interfere in their religion. So people are sceptical in the less secured and socio-political environment and their mistrust is widened if some confidence building measures are not taken into account and a good rapport is not taken place. So in advance, some trust-building measures must be taken before or after entering the community. In order to gain legitimacy and wider acceptance NGOs must adapt some trust building measures to come to terms with the community, they want to serve.

Modern-day community mobilization techniques and approaches evolved from four major sources.

1. In 1968, Paulo Frier developed **Activist Participatory Research** the core values of which were dialogue like Socrates and joint research that helped people raise their awareness and confidence level thereby empowering them to take action towards the solution of their problem. This technique was limited to help the underprivileged and take political action. So in modern day its significance and contributions lie in its emphasis on the creativity and capability of poor people, but what organizations should do is to play the role of catalysts and facilitators.

2. Gordon Conway and colleagues in 1987 developed a technique called "Agroecosystem Analysis" which draws on systems and ecological thinking combined with the analysis of systems, analysis of space and time, flows and relationships regarding productivity, stability, sustainability and equity. Its relevance lies in modern-day use as a technique that draws mapping and diagramming and the use of scoring and ranking to assess innovations.

3. "Modern Applied Anthropology" is another approach to capitalize on furthering rural peoples' knowledge to help professionals and researchers avoid jumping to conclusions by building people trust and confidence to establish rapport and to draw farmers to agriculture research. Their activities were taken as experiments in the context of risk-prone, complex and diverse farming system. So here the main focus was to put farmers on research and do experiments.

4. The RRA: "Rapid Rural Appraisal" is still in use and mobilizer and surveyors, researchers get insights into rural people livelihood conditions and thereby proposing and devising strategies to address their needs. In modern-day, most RRAs come from the disastrous situation, like natural disasters and manmade disasters, like a civil war, internally displaced peoples (IDPs) and refugees' crises, though it's a technique that can be used in health, agriculture sector research, non-formal education and forestry. The RRA will be further discussed in a separate heading.

Following are techniques that can be adapted in order to win peoples' support and acceptance. But first, we have to look at how these techniques evolved through history.

The history dates back to 2300 BC old tradition of Greek when great philosopher Socrates used to imply the method of people's participation towards increasing their information and knowledge regarding their circumstances. He used to gather people around him to transform their information into knowledge and motivate people to speak their opinions about their own socio-political, cultural, economic environment and he kept on asking people the "why" question. The method he used was the first community motivational method to make people speak and question their own attitude and behaviour and also regarding their socio-political environment to bring improvements. His motivational campaign of the masses provoked the existing political leaders and he was poisoned to death. So in the recorded history, Socrates was the first man to use techniques of people's motivation to gather people around him and ask their opinions about circumstances, both internal and external to question their existence for a purpose far better than what was existed at his time.

All these techniques and participatory approaches give rise to modern-day community mobilization techniques that believe in peoples' knowledge, their greater participation regarding their livelihood, socio-economic, political, cultural, environmental and technological conditions. Modern techniques of community mobilization and participatory approaches have the core democratic values of "for the people, of the people and by the people".

Modern techniques about people's motivation to question their own existence and their surroundings: With the growth of NGOs, conventional techniques were replaced by modern ones. The dissatisfaction with conventional technique of "Rural Development Tourists, Robert Chambers (1992) and Andrea Cornwall, Irene Guijt and Alice Welboum (1993), that failed to deliver tangible benefits to the beneficiaries due to its imposed decisions and inherent biases that either ignored rural people in their problem analysis or tended to dig out the real problems people were facing. So in the process, rural people's problem and poverty remained hidden and rural development tourist-packed up and returned with their own perceptions leaving the rural poor people just as to look at them. So the relationship between the primary stakeholders and project implementers was not more than onlookers and tourist relationship. The second reason for dissatisfaction with the conventional techniques was the tedious and inaccurate method of questionnaire methodology. This method led to the formation of new techniques that were participatory in nature, accurate in findings and involving those for whom the project meant. Modern techniques of the participatory approach to community development incorporated people's knowledge about their circumstances and were taken at the heart core of any developmental project. The core value of conventional techniques was imposed decision while modern techniques incorporated the democratic values as "of the people, for the people and by the people". Because problems spur by their circumstances, and they must be involved in the process of problems identification, analysis and devising strategies to solve them. In modern techniques, the relationship between the primary stakeholders and project implementers goes deeper by building their trust to establish rapport.

Diagram No 3, comparison;

Conventional and modern participatory techniques:

Contemporary and conventional participatory tools and technique(comparison)   By Iqbal Shah
https://reforgenonprofit.blogspot.com/

Conventional Techniques core values	Modern particpatory techniques core values
Dictated development process	Believe in people / indigenous knowledge
One Sided approach	Participatory in nature
Biased decision	Un-biased decision making process
Believe in dictatorial values	Believe in democratic values
Inaccurate data collection and survey	Accurate data collection and survey based on best practices of data collection tools
Imposed decisions	Ensure people participation in decision making process
Short terms projects	Long term sustainable projects

A comparison.... by Iqbal Shah — Modern and conventional participatory techniques

Umbrella tools and techniques

Participatory Approaches to Community Development

Participatory Approaches:

In today's changing the world, developmental programmes and project are launched in a specific sector for a certain specific community in a time-bound manner with community active participation resulting in tangible and intangible benefits to them.

Target community involvement in different phases of the project:

The phenomenon to involve people in the inception process to project development and then onward from project to monitoring and evaluation of the project are done in such a way to involve all the stakeholders, especially the primary stakeholders in the development/advocacy process. The process of community development is incomplete with the active involvement of the primary stakeholders, as for which the intervention logic is developed. And not only the process of development such as identification of the problem, the inception of intervention logic, the planning phase of the project, implementation and monitoring and summation and evaluation of as end result/product of the process. So from process to product (project inception to project goal achievement), all phases of the project are made participatory as to make the target community owns the end results. With people, involvement project cannot be made sustainable, long-lasting. People involvement brings not transparency and accountability in the process, but also the target community feels ownership for long-lasting sustainable results/impacts/goal.

Sustainability factor and people participation:

In this modern era of community development, intervening agencies are made bound by their donors to work for long-lasting sustainable impacts, so the intervening agency cannot ignore this sustainability factor as it makes the community own both failures and successes of the projects/programmes. Projects are owned by the community as they have involved from the very inception to evaluation phases of the intervention.

Different participatory techniques:

Different participatory techniques and tools are implied to ensure peoples' greater participation in these projects meant for them. Organizations play the role of catalyst and facilitators. Participatory approach invokes transparency, accountability, ownership, sustainability.

Community involvement:

Community participation is needed to ensure (1) people involved in the process of development; (2) and accountability on the part of an intervening agency, donors and primary stakeholders. Every intervention in the community living, working and livelihood conditions need to be participatory in nature, as this practice inspires support, involvement and feedback. Greater participation and involvement on the part of primary stakeholders can ensure due diligence. It also ensures accountability in humanitarian and development contexts and these further ads to the trust-building measures between the intervening agency and the primary stakeholders.

Participatory Learning and Action:

An umbrella term, "Participatory Learning and Action", is used for these mobilization and participatory techniques. These participatory tools and techniques aim at mobilizing the target community so as to ensure greater participation, leadership skills development. These tools and techniques also involve the marginalized, women and girls of the community, local leadership, indigenous community and youth. Some of good techniques and tools are Experiential Learning Cycle, Problem Identification Analysis Priority Setting (PIAPS), Participatory Rural Appraisal (PRA), Rapid Rural Appraisal (RRA), and Participatory Learning Method, Participatory Action Plan, Farming Systems Research, Baseline Survey, Interviews, Questionnaires, Focused Group Discussion. See the following diagram.

Diagram No 4

Community Mobilization Techniques:

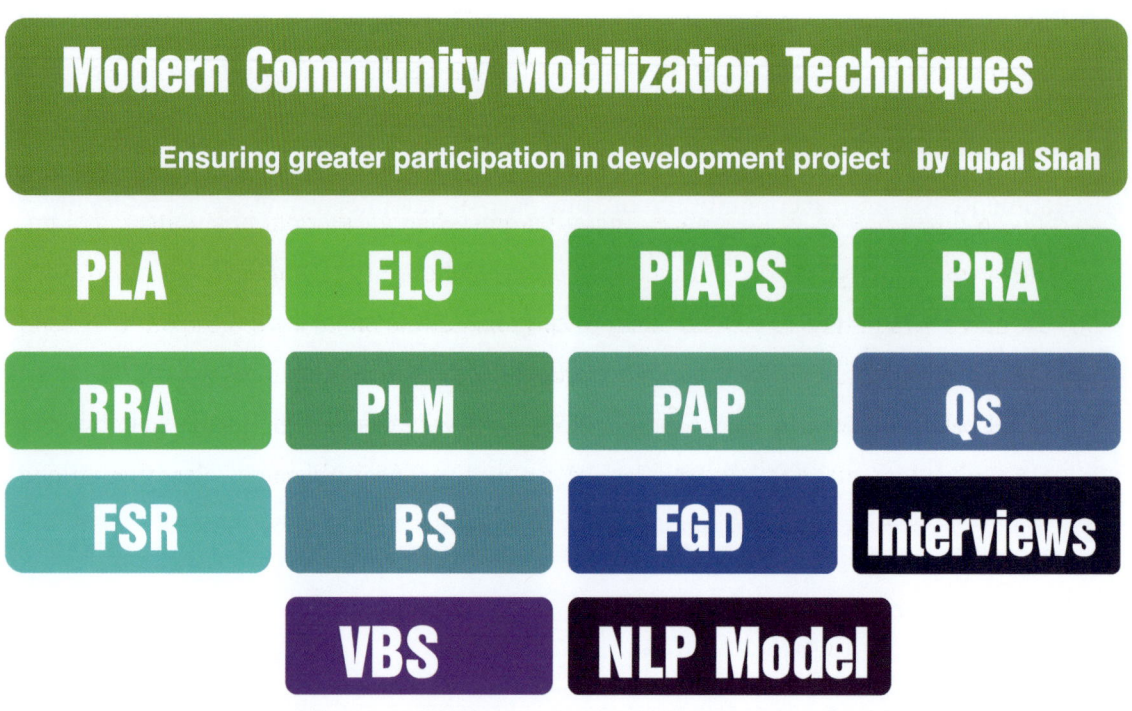

The history of community mobilization dates back to 2300 BC old tradition of Greek when great philosopher Socrates used to imply the method of people's participation towards increasing their information and knowledge regarding their circumstances. He used to gather people around him to transform their information into knowledge and motivate people to speak their opinions about their own socio-political, socio-ethical, cultural, economic environment and he keeps on asking people the "why" question. The technique he used was an authentic technique for people motivation and he used to encourage people to speak up their minds and ask questions and he used this community motivational method to make people speak and question their own attitude and behaviour and also regarding their socio-political environment to bring improvements. The method he tested provoked people mentally and thus they questioned their own socio-politico environment. His motivational campaign of the masses provoked the existing political leaders and he was poisoned to death. So in the recorded history, Socrates was the first man to use this technique of people's motivation to gather people around him and ask their opinions about their socio-politico environment from the ethical point of view and people questioned their existence for a purpose far better than what was existed at his time. First, he asked some ethical questions from some people and people used to gather around and participate in the discussion. There were three parts of this FGD (Focus Group Discussion), or three round of this discussion board that used to be spontaneous at that time as Socrates has no special place for FGD. In the first part, people used the present thesis in regard to the matter under discussion. In part two, antithesis used to be presented and Socrates used to play the role of a moderator. In the end, Socrates used, to sum up, the discussion by presenting the synthesis of the discussion. So it was a method used by philosopher Socrates to know people opinions and beliefs about some ethical topics prevailed at that time.

Socrates method is still used in modern-day as community mobilization technique for sustainable participatory community development, as Focus Group Discussion, Interview and VBS.

A Practical Guide to NGO and Project Management

Community mobilization techniques:

Philosopher Socrates technique of people motivation

Philosopher Socrates Community mobilization techniques:

Philosopher Socrates Technique:
by Iqbal shah

- Philosopher Socrates used to capitalize on people opinions and at the end of *FGD, presented his own to correct the situation
- Philosopher Socrates asked people why problem existed!
- At the end, Socrates used to sum up the discussion.
- People used to forward their answers based on what they used to believe

https://reforgenonprofit.blogspot.com/

*FGD/ Focus Group Discussion

Experiential Learning Cycle (ELC) Definition:

Participatory tools and techniques

ELC is community mobilization tool to analyze people experience about a problem by implying the core democratic values of "by the people, of the people and for the people" to make ground for the project to be implemented. The basis of ELC is the Socratic technique of peoples' transformation. Both inductive and deductive logic is used as to put community members to some specific experiences and use that specific experience and knowledge to correct weaknesses and capitalize on strengths for future similar experiences or to generalize those experiences and thereby transform oneself or the society.

Purpose of ELC :

ELC is a powerful tool in the context of community mobilization to get people on board to analyze the problems they faced or facing, take decisions regarding their solutions and act upon to solve them. This activity ensures people active participation in the process of development and avoids imposed decisions regarding their situations. The process moves in a cycle, starting from direct experience, reflecting on the experience, the generalization of experience and to its application.

Experience:
In this part of the cycle, the learner goes through new information that culminates in his/her transformation to put forward a response to it.

Reflecting on Experience

This part of the cycle makes the learner/community to reflect on its experience to analyze the emerging or emerged problems. Reflecting on new information that people transform into knowledge can lead to better-informed decisions.

Generalization about the Experience:

Both deductive and inductive logic are used to move from specific experience to generalization and from general experience to the specific problem

Application:

In this part, people apply their experience based on new information and knowledge to find solutions to their specific problem that has been at the core of all other problem to make ground for a project to be implemented serving only one purpose.

Diagram ELC

PIAPS Technique:

Definition of PIAPS

Problem Identification, Analysis, Priority setting is the technique which makes the people involved in a community setting to identify problems that affecting them the most, do the analysis of them and set priority to be addressed in a project. Problems exist in a community but the community has to analyze the root causes of it and thus reaching a consensus that it's now the time to set priority to address the problem which is at the root cause of all other problems.

Types of problems:

Primary:

Primary problem is that complex problem of a specific community which gives rise to all other problem. It is at the analysis phase of PIAPS that people get set to explore that.

Secondary:

These are the problems which spring out from the root cause of the problem and usually less complex in nature and its effect upon society.

Tertiary:

They are the easiest and usually resolve and solve them with little efforts and resources.

Purpose of PIAPS:

The purpose and relevance of this technique are to prioritize problems to avoid the impression of imposed decision from influential and outside people and that they themselves have the knowledge of their socio-economic, political, environment and culture settings to identify, choose and implement a project. The pre-requisite for this technique is that people have the knowledge, live or familiar with the area.

Application of PIAPS:

The techniques are implied to empower the targeted community to vent their feelings and opinion about their current or emerging problems; do analysis and forward strategies and solutions to the priority problem which is at the root cause of all othe problems. So people are gathered to let them identify their problems, do the analysis of them and categorizing them into tertiary, secondary and at last, primary problems.

PIAPS Technique — by Iqbal Shah

- Problem Identification, Analysis, Priority Setting
- Problem identification
- Analysis of problems
- Priority setting

TOTE MODEL and its application

Application of TOTE (Test Out Test Exit) in Community/social mobilization context

In the problem analysis phase of the project, the community start using the TOTE model to find a solution to the problems. Different strategies to resolve the problem go through the test out and test exit exercise in order to find a feasible, cost-effective, time-bound, efficient, relevant and suitable strategy to solve the problem.

TOTE model is applied mostly in the planning phase of the project in order to ascertain whether a strategy is workable, efficient and cost-effective. When a community move from a problem state of affairs to the desired state of affairs (finding solution to the problem), TOTE is applied in order to find relevant and cost-effective strategy within means and resources to resolve the issue/ problem and strategy fills the gap between a problem state of affairs and desired state of affairs. Moving from problem state of affairs to the desired state of affairs (solution part) is called strategy. When the gap between problem state of affairs to the desired state of affairs is filled with steps to be taken to move this path, that part of the project is called strategy analysis, and when the gap is filled with a strategy consisting of steps to be taken (solution part of the project), that part of the project is called operational plan of the project and the operational plan carries steps to meet/achieve objectives.

So strategy analysis is done by using the TOTE model in order to arrive at the solution to the problem.

When strategy is broken apart in a systematic way to achieve objective, that part of the project is called operational plan, and when operational plan meets set objectives then that part of the project is called objective phase as in this phase objective/results are started counting and project results culminate in the achievement of overall goal of the project.

Problem to desired state of affairs

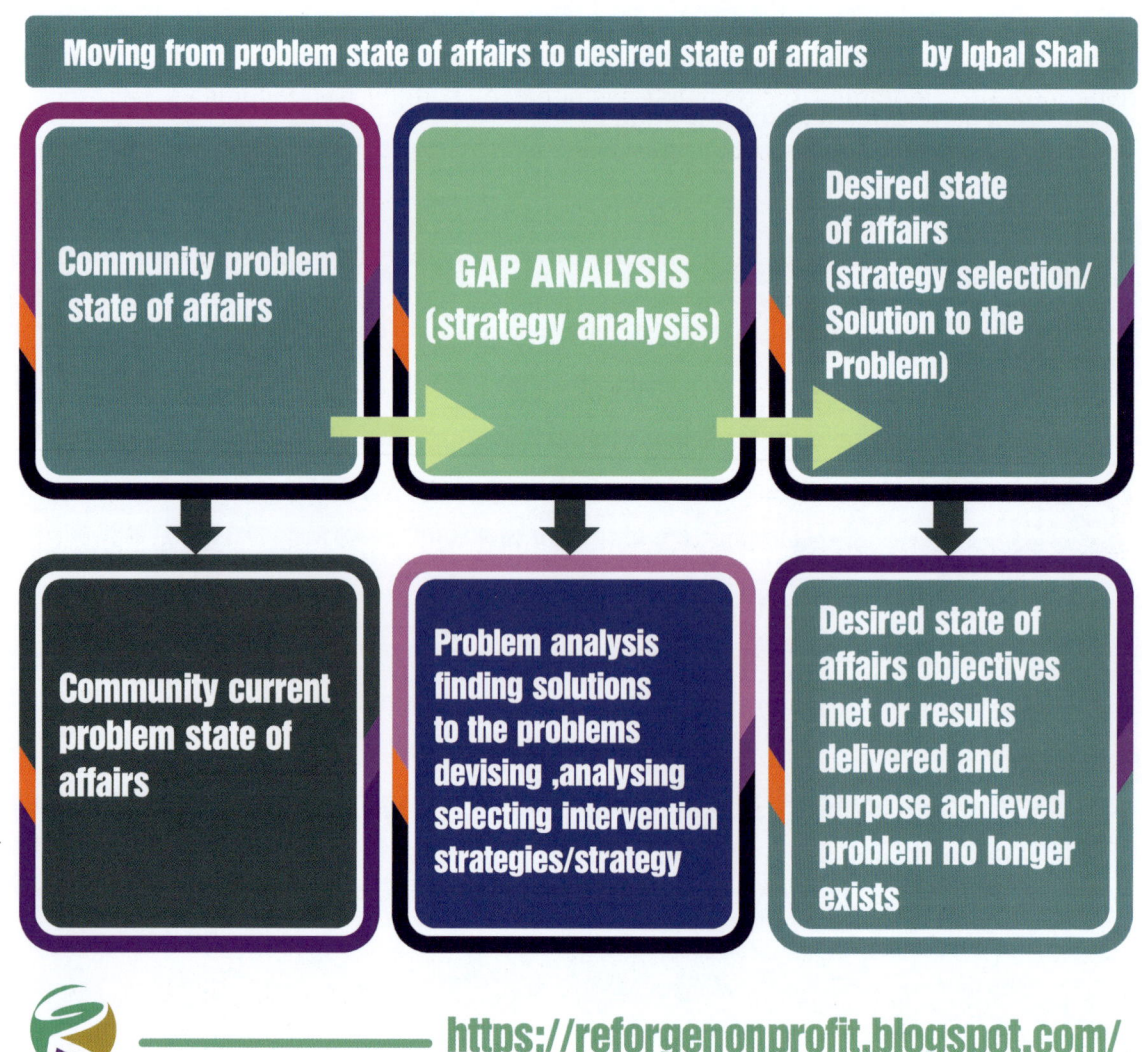

TOTE Model

When you put strategies to test out and test exit, relevant, feasible and cost-effective strategy is retained and other irrelevant strategies are discarded. A strategy is retained on the basis of its feasibility, relevance, cost-effectiveness, budget bound and suitability. The community at the planning phase of the project, exercise TOTE model so that better solutions to the problem is found within means and resources. Test out and test exit is repeated and this exercise results in a strategy that is feasible, relevant, suitable, within means and resources and sustainable. On the basis of strategy, the operational plan is prepared so as to intervene to resolve the problem that the community identified through active community participation. TOTE model is applied in a community context to strategize in order to invoke active community participation to find solutions to the problem. This, in turn, ensures greater transparency and accountability as the intervening agency, donor agency and the primary stakeholders are actively involved in the whole process and are made responsible to each other through the application of such participatory tools and techniques. The application of TOTE Model to strategize inspires and ensures active community participation as the model calls for community indigenous knowledge to be combined with modern necessary tools and techniques to resolve the issue /problem.

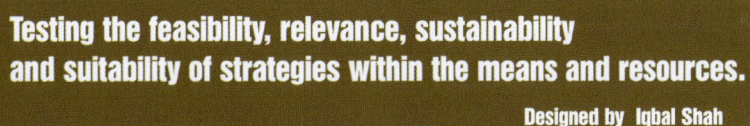

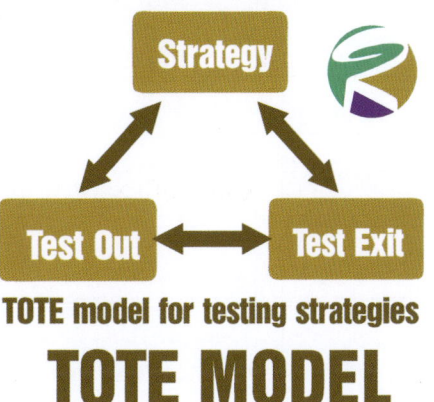

Motivating peoples using NLP Model

NLP Logical Model: -

Making an appropriate emotional appeal to people to act out

Defining NLP:

logical Model is a technique developed by Gregory Bateson (1972-1979) to gauge a person on the ladder of excellence pertaining to his/her environment, behaviour, capacity, value system, and ego/purpose/mission/identity regarding his/her life and further tie it up with the society as a whole.

Explanation of NLP

In the community context, it can be explained a system that intervenes where a community is fallen prey to the status quo and there seems no transformation on the part of the whole community as a unit. So an expert in NLP Logical Model sees the community on the ladder of excellence that where the problems lie. So the expert sees the ladder as to whether or not the problems lie with people physical and no-physical environment or their behaviour, or they lack capacity and need to be trained in some skills, or their value system is to be changed to bring about social change, or the people

Lack of proper direction towards realizing their goals and solve their problems and working towards them as one unit.

Purpose of NLP

The purpose of this technique is to bring about change in peoples' environment, behaviour, capacity building, belief system and overall goal /mission setting with a proper direction and guidelines to take them to move on the path of their change.

Application of NLP

The technique is applied to individual and community alike. Bottom to top and top-down approach is implied to move an individual or society towards realizing its goal and objective and to make them shun the impression from "cannot" to "can". Thus individual and society are transformed by studying deeply their ladder of excellence know where transformation is needed.

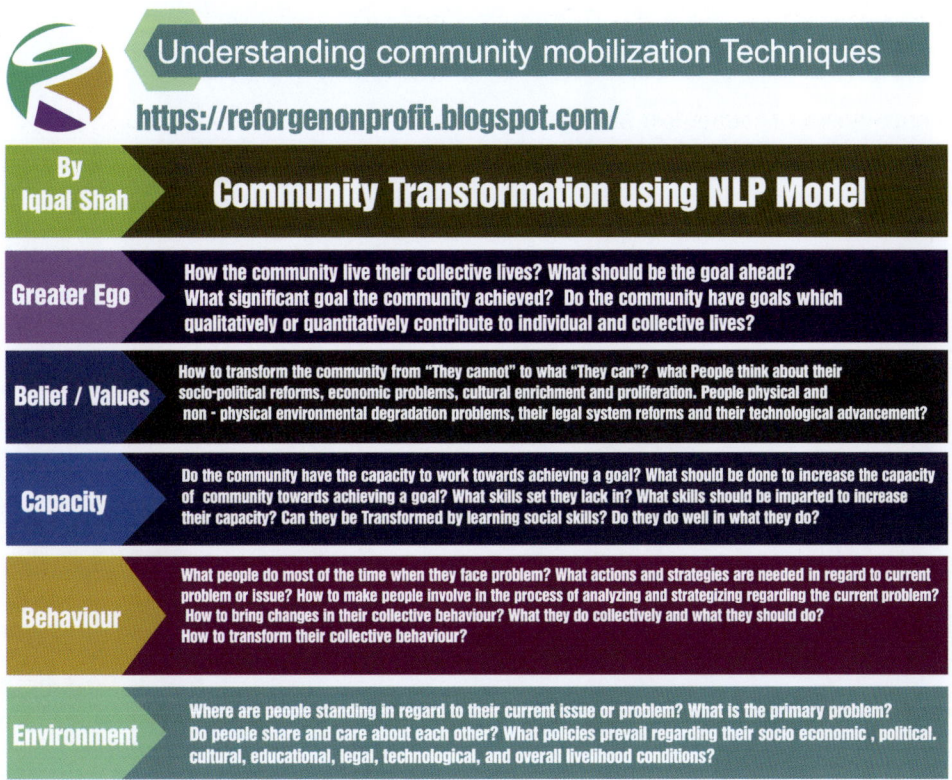

Motivating people using NLP Logical Model

As the following table shows which is not exhaustive that every level of logical model has its own practical and theoretical framework within which an individual or society has their own limitations and strengths, weaknesses and opportunities but it is the work of NLP expert practitioner or community mobilizer who has knowledge of it has to know them and make an individual or society to move on the path of success and remove barriers and hindrances that result in their limiting movement. So the work of a NLP Practitioner and community mobilizer is to play the role of facilitator to change an individual and society environment in which they live and behave, change their behaviour if required, build their capacity to achieve whatever they want to, strike a change in their value and belief systems, and change the society from "we cannot" to "we can".

Seasonal Calendar:

Defining Seasonal Calendar

It's a time bound recurring pattern of cyclic calendar activities of rural peoples. It can be as lengthy as a month or as short as an hour.

Purpose:

This mode of cyclic activities relates people with their environment that how much a time span can affect or contribute to their productive activities?

Seasonal calendar relevance to the project:

The seasonal pattern analysis can better identify peoples' peak hours or months that contribute to their living conditions and climatic changes and off-season can affect their lives by having no other means of livelihood or in search of or adapting other strategies to sustain lives. The analysis of these patterns can further add to the knowledge of implementing agency that how and in what manners people adapt to their circumstances during the off-season or during the season when there are harvesting and sowing seasons on their shoulders? While doing analysis, the implementing agency can better understand and feel the pressure of stakeholders during their peak time to opt for other alternative livelihoods. This analysis is better in case the implementing agency launches a project of other alternative livelihood conditions.

The seasonal calendar is just to respect people indigenous livelihood conditions and thereby creating other alternative livelihood conditions, it is not to disturb their peak hours, seasons where they are busy in harvesting and cutting their crops or seasons where they care most for their crops, community raring and some other tasks they undertake for creating their livelihood conditions.

When the staff of intervening agency enters a community, they should know the seasonal calendar of the community concerned, as this would lead to better understanding and rapport building. As for example, the community would not listen to the intervening agency for creating alternative livelihood conditions when they are busy in harvesting and cutting their crops. The intervening agency needs to know people/community seasonal calendar in order to build their trust and rapport to invoke their greater participation.

Seasonal Calendar Diagram

Seasonal Calendar
By Iqbal Shah

https://reforgenonprofit.blogspot.com/

Temporal set of time with which a specific community leads its life in specific environment that reveals the following productive and unproductive patterns.

People's productivity in terms of economic activities as labour, harvesting, agri-based, industry based, so as to allow people peak season move smoothly and be productive to their maximum.

People's un-productivity in terms of economic activities as their health conditions with climatic change, their unbalance expenditure on their livelihood conditions and the strategies that they adopt to meet their unbalance income and expenditure requirements.

So the patterns of life with which the people live, is respected and taken care of. In peak seasons, labour consumes most of the time of rural people as people are busy are busy in making livelihood and they look to other livelihood conditions with minimum attention as these alternatives are new and take time which they cannot afford. So people are busy in making livelihood and the patterns suggest saving for off seasons in which they economically un-productive

So organizations that enter to intervene for a specific project in that community must take into account people labour demand at the time of intervention, so that people demand for labour and income generation should not be effected, otherwise they would not afford to try other livelihood alternatives or something else.

RRA (Rapid Rural Appraisal):

Definition of RRA

RRA is systematic activity outside in the rural areas by a certain multi-disciplinary team for gathering information on the basis of which some hypotheses are formulated for further in-depth analysis about rural life. The team is composed of such persons who are experts in their specialized disciplines. So in this type of rural appraisal, a multidimensional approach is implied in order to ascertain certain types of data, correlated in its nature to the overall rural life of the people. So the scenarios that come into focus are multi-dimensional in their character as it incorporates all aspects or certain aspects of rural life.

So different perspectives with multidimensional disciplines, as for example, rural economy, agriculture, rural culture, different livelihood conditions, people attitude and behaviour, gender roles and its sensitivity are taken care of.

The technique is based on the following points and perspectives:

Interview design to obtain information

Taking sampling as techniques to further explore some objectives

To obtain quantitative data in a short time frame

Group discussion, interviews including focused group discussion

Direct site observation and obtaining information

Using secondary data sources

Characteristics of RRA

It can be as simple as to know the conditions of people in disastrous situations or can be as broad as to incorporate all sectors of rural people on which their livelihoods are based.

Different perspectives come into focus by implying different techniques and sector specialists.

Hypotheses are formulated and tested in the fields that provide for further study to explore some sector or all of them more in detail in order to reach conclusions about rural peoples' livelihood conditions.

Different research techniques are used in order to ascertain data collection and data analysis, as observations, semi-structured interview, focused group study, questionnaire method, baseline survey, stakeholders' analysis by incorporating their opinions and knowledge to further include them in projects for the areas.

Chambers in his book "Chambers, R, (1980), Rural Development: Putting the Last First, Harlow, England" [9] calls RRA a "fairly-quick and fairly- clean" appraisal unlike the fast and careless studies that he termed as "quick and dirty studies" as "Rural Development Tourist" method and the slow one he describes as "long and dirty" as early questionnaire method.

Application of RRA

The RRA technique which incorporates many good techniques within itself as mentioned above is widely used in agriculture sectors, non-formal education, health, disasters, as natural disasters like flood and earthquakes and manmade, as the civil war, IDPs and refugees' crises. In disastrous situations, RRA is very useful to meet the requirements of internally displaced peoples and refugees who take refuge in another country due to civil war broke out in their own country. RRA is used as a quick method to know the peoples' condition in those situations in order to meet their livelihood requirements.

RRA is used as a quick research method to improve upon rural people livelihood conditions.

RRA is unbiased in contrast to other methods which were or are biased in neglecting the poorest people and meeting a few influential and also ignoring women and the marginalized in their studies.

RRA Diagram

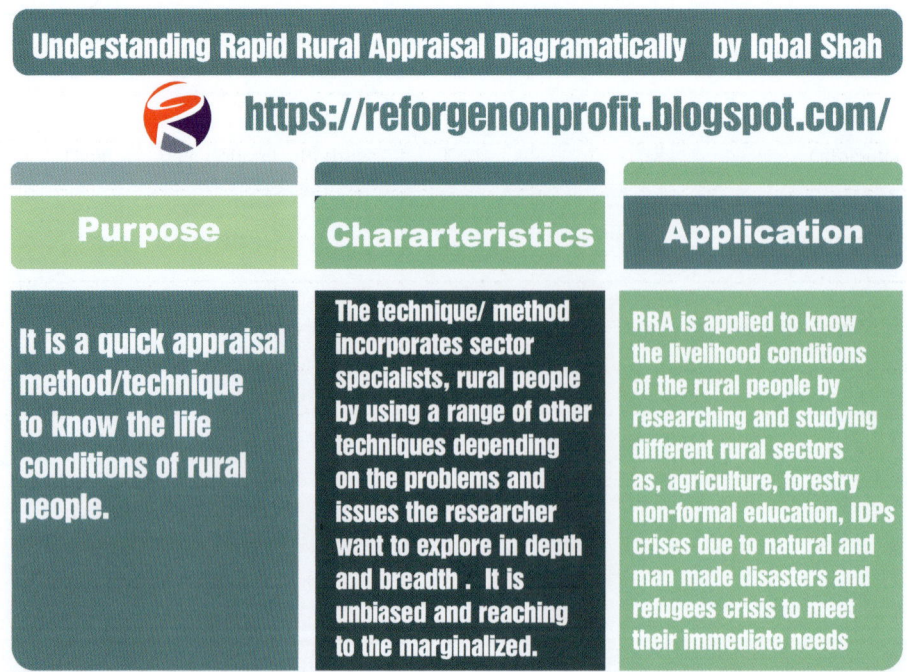

Problem Tree/Web:

It's a brainstorming technique to mobilize the community to know the cause and effect relationship of their problems. This technique is better applied to when the community has been mobilized to establish a cause and effect relationship of the problem. The time then comes to prepare the community through external facilitation as done in community mobilization process, to draw cause and effect relationship in a tree-like a shape starting from cause to effect up to the top so that a real primary problem has to be identified that perpetuated all other secondary and tertiary problems. So it is a participatory technique involving all stakeholders to go into depth and breadth of the real primary problem to be addressed later in the project after doing objectives analysis. Objective analysis is different from problem analysis by drawing a problem tree, but when the stakeholders are done with this exercise, they then find solutions and adapt strategies to solve the primary problem by doing objectives analysis. In the objective analysis, the cause and effect relationship is turned into solutions and strategies, and when the cause is removed, the effect disappears. In an objective analysis, causes are replaced by solutions and strategies thereby effects disappear with these proposed strategies.

Pre-requisites

Problem Tree/Web:

It is a participatory technique involving all stakeholders.

A good facilitator is required to facilitate the course of drawing problem tree/web.

Stakeholders themselves go through this exercise.

The exercise is done after the application of a series of community mobilization techniques to gather around, build the trust of the community, rapport building with a community of an external agency, getting community support as to prepare the ground to launch the project.

Community learns to identify their complex problems, analyze, proposing strategies and solutions to address their main problem.

A good facilitator must guide the people to know that "What is a problem?" "What is the cause of it?" and "What the effects are?"

It's a good process ensuring people to be equipped with to identify problems and get to know the cause and effect relationship of these problems and finding solutions to solve these problems.

So the technique empowers people to know the complex problems that they are facing and thereby minimize their dependency syndrome to look to outsiders to come, intervene and proposed a solution to their problem. The technique empowers people to capitalize on their own sources within the community.

Cause and Effect Relationship:

The process of cause and effect relationship in a community meeting goes like the following:

Capitalize on rapport:

Organize people to focus on problems:

Target community presents a problem:

Facilitator/community mobilizer/social organizer draws a tree trunk:

The cause comes forth and the root is added to the problem tree.

Continue on adding roots to the problem tree and writing secondary causes over the primary ones.

Then draw branches for the tree to write effects on them, secondary over the primary ones.

Then meeting comes to an end by identifying the primary problem.

Then comes the time to go through the process of objectives analysis when the community finds solutions to their problems.

Strategies are devised and solutions come forth from stakeholders to solve the problems. Indigenous knowledge is respected and is taken care of so that the community takes responsibility and ownership to what they are doing with regard to their problem and finding a solution to them.

Problem Tree/ Cause and effect relationship

The process of establishing cause and effect relationship
By Iqbal shah
https://reforgenonprofit.blogspot.com/

Hold a meeting and organize the community on the identification of problems

Tell them how to distinguish problems and their causes and effects

Draw a tree trunk and write problems on it

Ask the community why this problems exists?

Then add a tree root to trunk and write some causes that come forth from the community. Then secondary causes until the community explores as much as possible

If there are no more causes, then draw a branch of tree for each effect as a result of cause. This process continues until the community identify most of the effects.

Questionnaire Method

Understanding the questionnaire method:

This questionnaire method is a set of questions that are asked orally or in written to know about a particular living condition. It is one of the four methods of data collection, that is, (1) observation, (2) questionnaire, (3) interview and (4) focus group discussion or session. The questionnaire method can be both quantitative and qualitative. Questionnaire method was used in early research as a methodology to collect data in the field on a pre-hypotheses made basis using sampling, (purposive, as relating to a particularly specific purpose, for example, child labour). It was a method used to know community mindset about a particular problem, then those statistics that were collected, tabulated and conclusions were drawn up. Today this method is used for academic research purposes and also in some cases a purposive method in order to collect data about a particular problem in a specific community.

Emile Durkheim (1858 – 1917) introduced a structured questionnaire method in order to involve the respondent deeply and lowered the level of a researcher in the process. The product needs to be statistically tabulated, analyzed and a conclusion drawn upon. The researcher needs not to be personally involved there with the respondents as respondents are asked or can be asked through different communication channels like emails, post mail, face to face or using mobile or phone for the purpose.

Questionnaire type of data collection is used for different purposes, such as asking questions about customer satisfaction, knowing a particular living condition within a community, research paper/topic, etc.

This method gives ease to the interviewee (respondents) as it does respect his/her time and schedule and he or she is asked either orally or in written form. It can be either qualitative such as open-ended questions, primary data (documents) and structured interview or quantitative such as all respondents are asked the same type of questions and they are tabulated, analyzed and results drawn up

Characteristics of the questionnaire method:

(Questionnaire method):

Questions are in written form based on some hypotheses to be distributed in the target group in order to collect data about a particular problem.

A questionnaire is also set in oral form and all questions are asked orally to know a particular life condition.

Questions are categorized and the set of questions are further analyzed and tabulated.

The questions set in the method needs to be simple, precise and easy to respond.

The method is tedious as the researcher has to distribute the questionnaire amongst a specific community on which his/her research is based.

The method needs to respect the seasonal calendar of the respondents.

The questionnaire distributed is then collected and statistics are tabulated.

The accuracy of data collected through questionnaire method can be undermined if accurate data and information are held back by the community.

So the information collected through questionnaire method can be biased either by ignoring the outreached, marginalized community or if the community hold back some important information on the basis of which the researcher wants to draw conclusions on.

It can be corrected through semi-structured interviews, focused group discussions in order to collect correct data to draw on conclusions.

Questions can be open-ended for some qualitative data collections, multiple-choice question, yes or no questions (dichotomous) scaling and pictorial question

Questions are asked as using channels; (1) face to face, (2) through email, (3) mobile or phone questions, (4) post mail questions.

Designing a questionnaire:

The subject matter of the questionnaire needs to be determined first, as what you are going to research or ask the question on?

The researcher needs to be flexible to try different options while asking respondents.

Know your questionnaire well in advance as to how to ask which question; either open-ended or closed-ended?

Know your respondents as this will make you use the right technique to ask your respondents.

A researcher needs to decide a session with respondents while respecting their seasonal calendar.

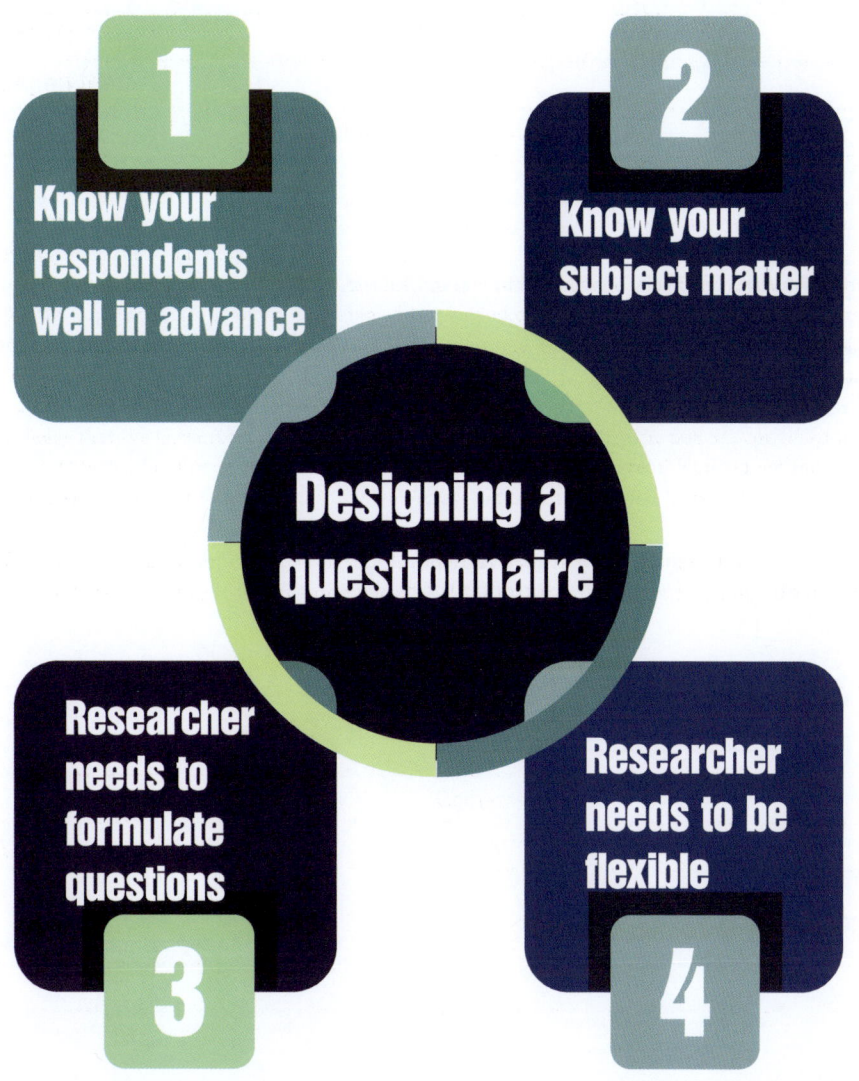

Interview:

In a community mobilization context:

An interview is an interaction with a purpose (one to one or more persons involved), designed to help you gather information through verbal conversation and non-verbal cues about people's environment, behaviour, capacity, attitudes and assumptions/perceptions of activities in a specific community.

Four points agenda of the interview:

It has four points' agenda;

Gather information about a person or persons for a specific purpose.

The analysis of that information gathered through verbal conversation and non verbal cues.

Taking decision on the basis of that analysis that whether it serves the purpose or not?

And at last to retain or reject.

Interview Process

Interview Process — By Iqbal Shah
https://reforgenonprofit.blogspot.com/

- Now draw conclusion and make a decision in favour or disfavour about the person interviewed. Avoid hasty generalizations about the person or community.

- Select question base on job description. Question are set well in advance to augment the flow of interview ; and some supplementary questions can also be asked.

- Analyze those information gathered during the interview process.

- Gather information during the interview information about a person's aptitude, environment, behaviour and capacity.

Village Baseline Survey (VBS):

The post defines and explains different types of surveys but elaborates more and keeps the focus on the Village Baseline Survey. There are different types of surveys, such as customer satisfaction surveys, employees' benefits and satisfaction surveys, trend surveys, market surveys, brand awareness surveys, etc. A survey is based on certain questions that are asked from respondents about a particular product or life conditions that either impede the living conditions or strengthen the effectiveness of certain actions taken to improve those conditions. Here the question arises as what is the difference between survey and questionnaire then? In a survey, a set of questions are asked from the respondents to ascertain respondents' opinions, experience, knowledge and actions pertaining to certain livelihood/living conditions with a purpose in mind to put answers to statistical tabulation and analysis and thereby draw conclusions from it. Though the questionnaire is a set of questions (oral or written) asked for the purpose of surveys.

Defining VBS

VBS is a quick form of village survey to know the livelihood conditions of a specific village or cluster of villages.

Purpose of VBS

Commonly village baseline survey VBS is conducted in order to know the problems of a specific village for project intervention.

VBS

It is baseline because it keeps the very basic into account starting from a minor one to old age vulnerable, men, women, children, infants, and adults and record minor problem to the big one. It records villagers' livelihood conditions, their economy, social and political awareness, their rights and duties, their daily routine living condition, demographic situation, health hygiene, population welfare and control, their community infrastructure, education(formal and non-formal), their agriculture, horticulture and forestry, mother and child health, their professions, offseason migratory trends, access to market, people income generation sources, access to clean drinking water, peoples' access to basic facilities and recreation, peoples' way of solving basic village problems, youth way of life, the impacts of unemployment, illiteracy, crimes on the life of the villagers, infants mortality and violence against women, bonded and forced labour.

So these problems and similar others are explored in the baseline survey to capitalize on peoples' strengths, get to know peoples' weaknesses and make plans to intervene.

The survey is usually conducted on written format using participatory methods so that indicators are developed against which project objectives are monitored and evaluated and strategies and activities are checked for effectiveness.

ter a baseline survey, one or more primary problems are selected for further in-depth analysis.

Participatory approaches are applied in a given community living/livelihood condition to reach a consensus on a particular problem as identified in the problem analysis phase of the project. As in the baseline survey, problems are identified and the community reaches a consensus to put a solution to them. The community leadership skills are further refined in the community mobilization and organization phase so that community as a whole is able to build consensus to solve a problem. So problems selected at the village baseline survey phase are analyzed and strategies to address them are explored to move forward from problem state of affairs to the desired state of affairs.

Participatory approaches are applied in a given community living/livelihood condition to reach a consensus on a particular problem as identified in the problem analysis phase of the project. As in the baseline survey, problems are identified and the community reaches a consensus to put a solution to them. The community leadership skills are further refined in the community mobilization and organization phase so that community as a whole is able to build consensus to solve a problem. So problems selected at the village baseline survey phase are analyzed and strategies to address them are explored to move forward from problem state of affairs to the desired state of affairs.

Characteristics of Village Baseline Survey:

It is comprehensive as it incorporates all or some of the impression and prompts of nearly all sectors pertaining to a village living and livelihood conditions.

Sector problem is identified by involving the community and its leadership.

Participatory approaches are adopted to involve the community and their leadership to identify problems faced by that specific village.

Leadership and problem-solving skills are imparted so that a comprehensive analysis of the problem is done within the village.

The intervening agency uses all communication channels in the locality to make local community involved in the process of the village baseline survey.

The intervening agency plays the role of a catalyst and leaves the whole takes its natural course. It facilitates the local community to be involved in the process of analyzing the problems and strategizing to put solutions to them.

The agency respects the seasonal calendar of a village in focus. The schedule and time of the local community are taken care of as these people are not available at peak time /hours.

The agency makes all the phases of the project participatory to inspire people' trust, transparency and accountability in the project.

The intervening agency makes it a win/win situation for all the stakeholders so that they are able to know the intervention logic in order to ensure transparency, and accountability in the project and win people trust for their greater involvement in all the phases of the intervention logic(project).

UNDERSTANDING VILLAGE BASELINE SURVEY

https://reforgenonprofit.blogspot.com/

DESIGNED BY IQBAL SHAH

- Tabulate statistics in a coherent way. Draw conclusions on the basis of these findings and devise strategic plan of action to be undertaken in the intervention or project. Motivate and mobilize people as much as possible to make them stick to and gather on their strengths.

- Paper work, questionnaire development about thematic area for project Intervention, sector like, agriculture, forestry, education, economy, living conditions health hygiene.

- Select a sector for further exploration, put the sector problems into in-depth analysis, gather information as much as possible, identify indicators for the project Intervention to be later on checked monitored and evaluated during the project.

- Transect walk observation, paper filing in, meeting target people and knowing Their livelihood conditions and asking questions written in baseline survey format prepared for the purpose.

Need Assessment Survey

Definition of NAS

Need assessment survey is a kind of survey meant for a specific community in order to assess what their needs are and how they can be met? So it is a kind of survey that explores the people unmet needs and entails further to intervene with a strategic plan of action by involving that specific community to meet these unmet needs. A way of gauging opinions, assumptions, needs, key issues, and/or assets within a defined community.

Desires and needs are classified so as the community is able to meet its unmet needs. The intervening agency (NGO) plays the role of a catalyst and makes people explore the genuine needs that they could not meet as they were notably mobilized and organized to take action to meet the unmet needs. The intervening agency (NGO) takes care of the mobilization and organization portion of the NAS survey, as the agency needs to mobilize and organize the community in regard to ascertaining its needs. The community leadership build consensus and leadership skills are further refined to differentiate between desires and needs, and needs are further classified into primary and secondary needs. Primary needs are taken care of first followed by secondary needs.

Purpose of NAS

The purpose of need assessment is to ascertain those unmet needs of a specific community by holding discussion sessions with some already prepared questions regarding that community in order to propose strategies to fulfil these needs. In order to go deep into the needs assessment of the specific community, use your first hand primary and secondary data about that community, collect information as much as possible so that needs and interests of the marginalized and outreached are addressed and met. Try to explore the community expectations from the implementer, the impacts upon the lives of people, especially the marginalized, by fulfilling their needs, people contributions (tangible or intangible) towards the project and project long term sustainability.

So the purpose of needs assessment survey is to explore more about peoples' needs by researching, field visits, and holding discussions with the concerned community, reaching out to the marginalized and outreached so that fulfilling these needs the community must reach its true potential, or as Maslow says, self-actualization, but keeping in view the needs and desires separate.

As for example, we need water in our village, as women used to bring water far from this village (need expressed). We desire high paid employment (desire expressed).

Need assessment survey is used to identify people' needs, key issues concerning their livelihood conditions, and ascertaining what people hopes are and what they can contribute to.

CHAPTER FOUR

NGO FINANCIAL MANAGEMENT

A sound system of financial management is a good practice for NGOs management staff, especially the chief executive to be familiar with all financial procedures and good practices in today world greater responsibility upon their shoulders from donors and stakeholders. Sound managerial skills in financial management ensure financial accountability both internally and externally to donors and stakeholders, but bring sustainability to the organization in its long term relationship with donors and internal accountability. History shows that only those organizations sustained their credibility and survived when they got good financial practices in place. Understanding financial records and their analysis keep the managers on a strong footing to build a relationship with donors for a future project. The analysis of these good financial systems-ensures managers that how his/her organization heading towards and how finances are to be managed for their credibility and have long term relationship with donors and stakeholders. So for an

Characteristics of Good Finance Practices

Bookkeeping is in place and proper records are maintained.

Budget monitoring reports are timely passed on to donors.

Trial balance, accrual record, cash flow and balance are taken care of.

Good books keeping practices are in place.

Bank statements, BRS (Bank Reconciliation Statement), staff salary sheet and other bank transaction ready to be audited internally and externally by the donors and auditor reports and opinions are taken care of.

Proper finance SOPs must be followed to bring credibility to the organization.

A deficit in income and expenditure must be avoided to the maximum.

Financial TORs with the donors must be followed to ensure that expenditure does not exceed the income.

All finance documentation must be properly in place.

Bank statements, cheque book record and stubs, payment voucher against invoices must be in order to be audited internally and externally by the donors.

A good internal control mechanism based on proper SOPs must be in place in order to minimize the chances of stealing, mishandling and misuse and abuse of the organization's assets. The organization employees' manual is a good guide policy guide to make employees know the dos and don'ts of the organization.

A good accountancy procedure must be followed to avoid mistakes and that ensure maximum accuracy.

Budget enlists those activities of the project that incur cost It is that itemized line by line and code by code activities list that incurred cost and estimates for the project to achieve its objectives. After TORs are developed, budgetary procedures agreed upon between the donor and the NGO are followed and complied with so as to complete the project within stipulated cost.

Donors don't want to:

Spend the fund outside the agreed TORs.

Spent funds on gifts.

Spend funds on unauthorized travel.

Spend funds lobbying, social activities, amusement,

Monthly budget is prepared so as to know whether or not the expenditure is in line with the agreed funding agreement. As the following table shows that that line items expenses are recorded on the left specified columns and the variances as noticed under budget or over budget are recorded on the right side of specified columns. Keeping such records ensure that funds are to be spent on agreed finance TORs between the donor and NGO. See the detail table in chapter 4 on finance format and procedures.

Account System:

Every NGO largely depends on a system of accounting that ensures a proper bookkeeping system so that the inflow and outflow of funds are to be recorded properly in books specified.

Accounts Auditing

Internal audit:

This is usually done by the board of director or a nominated person to ensure that the funds have been spent on agreed TORs with the donor and no discrepancy is found, and if there is any excess, the board can advise and forward its opinion to take some corrective measures not to let it happen again in the future. The internal audit makes the organization to find any discrepancies and correct them. This is usually done to ensure that all documentary proofs are available for the external audit to take place and if there are any discrepancies, they may be corrected.

External audit

This type of audit is done through a professional government registered chartered accountant to see;

The revenue and expenditure of an organization.

The expenditure according to donor and organization's agreement.

Assets, depreciation, liabilities, (current and past), year around

Does the chartered accountant give his/her expert opinion about how the finance and account system can be further improved?

Chartered Accountant has to see that whether or not all financial and account SOPs were followed?

This external audit document usually done at the end of the year is very important because nearly all donors see previous audit report as pre-requisite to approve of a project presented by that organization. The opinion of the external auditor is not ignored by the donor and many instances can result in disqualification if the auditor's opinion about the organization is not that much good enough and fails to qualify donor's standard of account accuracy. External auditor's remarks, "Qualified", "Disqualified" or need improvement in areas as given in auditor's remarks.

Diagram No 38, Internal and external Audit:

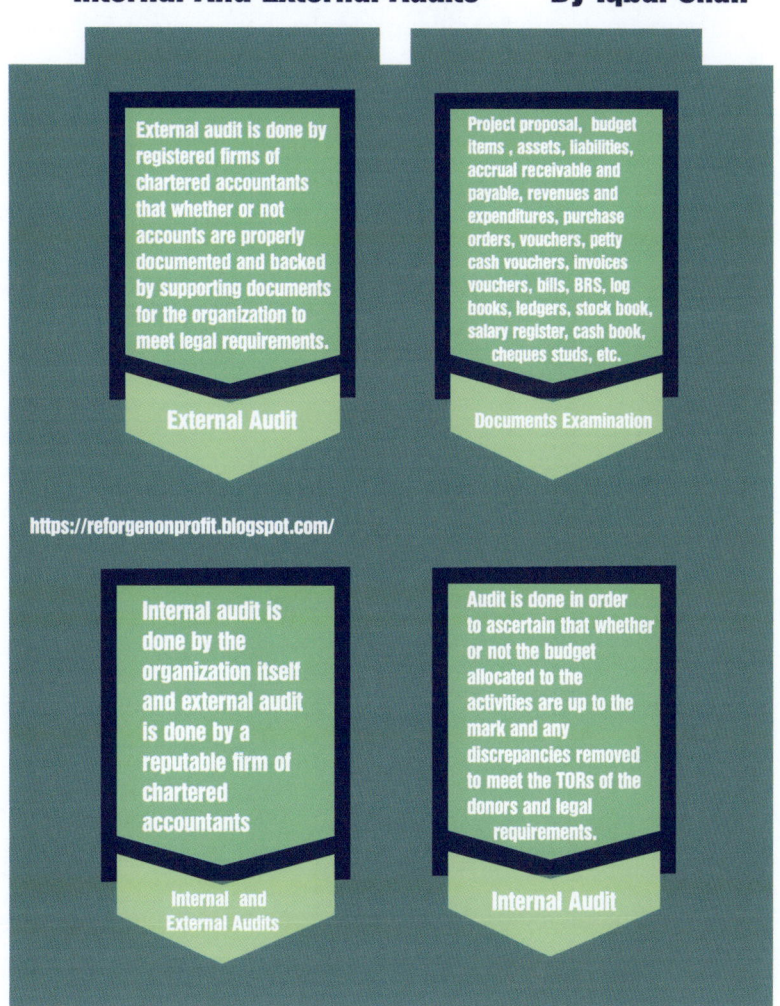

The external auditor will check the following document in order to reach some conclusion about the organization's financial record-keeping procedures and its soundness and give an opinion in a document called "audit report"

The documents the external auditor will see are:

Aims and objective of the organization written in its constitution.

Finance TORs agreed upon by the donor and organization.

A budget of the project in progress or completed.

Proposal for the grant

Cash flow, income and expenditure statements

Cashbook, cheque book register, cheques stubs, bank statements and BRS.

Petty cash reconciliation, petty cash record, expense record, bills, voucher and invoices.

Bank deposits and withdrawals books/registers

Accruals, receivable and payable

Staff salary record and a tax deduction and deposit record of employees.

Assets registers

Stock book

Logbook

Fuel vouchers

Invoices in support of expenses made or things purchased.

At the end of an audit, the auditor asks for any discrepancies that exist in revenue, expenditure, accrual payable and receivable, the planned versus actual expenditure and revenue and the chief executive or the relevant staff give an explanation to justify them. If however, the auditor is not satisfied with their explanation, he wrote these in his/ her audit report and advises the organization that such discrepancies may not happen again that could compromise the organization's credibility. If however the accounts were found accurate, financial and budgetary protocols and procedures followed, proper bookkeeping maintained, accounts reconciled, the auditor opinion can be good enough to establish organization's credibility and the opinion ends with "Qualified".

Petty cash is that amount of money that can be in safe, one person responsible for it to be spent on small items for office supply on need basis. The cash is meant for small office things to be purchased with and not meant for any staff advances or loan. The chief executive nominates one person (can be finance officer or administrator) to handle petty cash, request petty cash and the cheques must be approved of by the nominated signatories to release petty cash, see payment vouchers against expenses, reimbursement and replenish it.

All purchases that are made through petty must be accompanied by purchase orders, payment vouchers and properly requisitioned by a person who needs a supply of things.

So petty cash is:

Small cash authorized by the chief executive to meet emergency or routine small office supply or needs.

One person is responsible for it to fill in request on a proper form for a Requisitioner or fill in by the Requisitioner himself/herself.

The petty cash must be in a safe place and access to it is not allowed except the person responsible for it.

If the person responsible sees that the petty cash is running out, he can replenish it by requesting a cheque duly signed by the signatories responsible for issuing cheques.

Proper records of petty request, reimbursement, and replenish and purchases against it, proofs accompanied and cheques copies are recorded.

_The handler of petty cash has to fill in shortage from his pocket if any shortage in petty cash box is noticed for which he or she has no explanation and proof of spending.

_A certificate is signed by the petty cash handler to manage it.

_Petty cash log is maintained by the handler to record all transactions and requests.

Diagram No 39, Petty cash terminology explained:

Understanding petty cash terminology — By Iqbal Shah

https://reforgenonprofit.blogspot.com/

Definition of Petty Cash	It is a small amount in cash paid for small day-to-today office expense
Replenish	Expenses are debited and cash credited to replenish petty cash, when we $100 in box (petty cash float) and buy some post stamps, letter dispatches, office cleaning materials and the amount goes down to $50. To make it again to $100, we have to sign a cheque of $50 from the person in authority to make it again to $100. This called replenish petty cash.
Petty Cash Request	The petty cash made on a proper format having written on it the money requested
Petty Cash Reimbursement	When you spend petty cash on small day- to -day office supplies, whatever you spend, you request the same amount to reimburse the petty cash to raise it to the same amount as authorised.
Petty Cash Top-Up	When you have $100 as petty cash float and spend $50 on small thing supplied to office, so top-up the exact amount $50 to make the total float to $100.
Petty cash Journal/ Ledger, log	Here the entry of debit and credit is made to make the transaction transparent, and whenever you go to the box of petty cash, you count check the receipts against the expenses and see if there is any cash over or short. So you look for the discrepancies and reconcile petty cash. The log contains the following information such as, date, receipts no, description, amount, deposited amount withdrawn, charged to, received by, approved by.

Purchases and Procurement:

A proper procedure must be in place to purchase office supply things by following protocols as mentioned below. There must be a good procurement policy in place to ensure that expendable and non-expendable assets which are purchased with a sound procurement/ purchase committee judgments based on requisition merit, quotation analysis by seeing market competitive trends so that the sole sourcing may be checked or minimize for services and goods required. As sole sourcing for services and goods may be, sometimes goes wrong if market competitiveness, price, quality is not properly checked. But it may be good enough to keep all those above-mentioned things in mind and also if a good marketing relationship has been established and does not of any exploitative nature. So in case of any exploitative sole sourcing, quotations obtaining and comparative bid statements analysis is the choice best to be pursued.

A proper purchase committee is to be nominated consisting at least of three persons to oversee all purchases made or going to be made. Every requisition must go through analysis by the purchase committee.

Everything that is bought for short term or long term must best serve the organization purpose.

Quotation for expendable (as office stationery, papers etc) and non-expendable assets, such as a car, computer, laptop furniture, etc) are taken from three suppliers and the best one supplier whose rate, quality, after-sale service, is chosen by the purchasing committee and a purchased order is placed to buy. The final voice of the chief executive prevails by consulting the purchase committee.

These fixed assets are then recorded in fixed assets register on a proper format called "fixed Assets Register"

The expendable assets are used according to the organization's different department requirements that are recorded and issued by filling in and submitting a proper requisition form duly signed by the Requisitioner, person handling these assets with the approval of the organization's chief.

A purchase committee of at least three persons must be formed to look after the matter of purchases and procurement. And every requisition for purchase must be duly signed by the members of the purchase committee. Every requisition that comes forth on a proper format must be examined by the purchase committee. The requisition must be signed by the Requisitioner, checking person to establish the need, finance officer and final approval of the chief executive.

Every purchase must be made according to set finance parameters and the amount should not exceed for which the purchase committee is authorized.

If the procurement exceeds the limit the set finance parameters, then a higher authority is approached over the purchase committee to approve of bills. Every asset that is purchased is drawn up to assets register.

Expendable assets are recorded on a separate asset register and issuance record is maintained thereof. So the procedure for purchase and procurement goes like the following:

Diagram No 40, Procurement process:

PROCUREMENT PROCESS OF AN ORGANIZATION — By Iqbal Shah

Requisition	Requisition is to be forwarded to the purchase committee for assests to be purchased following SOPs
Purchase Decision	The purchase committee examines the needs of assets requisitioned
Quoutation	Upon approval, atleast three quotations are obtained from the market
CBS	Comparative Bid Statement is prepared and supplier is selected for purchasing assests
CBS Analysis	supplier are chosen on the basis of their credibility,, price, quality and afetr sale service of product and payment conditions.
Purchase Order	Order are placed to the selected supplier on a proper format
GRN/GIRN	When assets and goods are arrived, they are properly inspected and Goods Inspection and Received Note is prepared and damage items are marked and returned to the supplier with GIRN report
Supplier Invoice	If the items and assets are found in good condition, the supply is accepted and payments is made on agreed terms and conditions
Assets Register	Assets are registered in their proper register thereafter
Cash Book Entry	Entry is made in cash book and purchase record is kept

https://reforgenonprofit.blogspot.com/

NGOs Account and Book Keeping

It is that part of an organization financial record standardized system which ensures that all revenue (funds coming in) and expenditure (funds going out) are properly maintained, records kept, proofs obtained to support revenue and expenditure. It is that part of an organization financial standardized routine keeping record that aims to ensure that revenues are properly accumulated and disbursed according to scheduled activities plan/ project operational plan.

A good accounting system ensures

Greater transparency to NGO's sound financial management.

That proofs/supporting documents are obtained against expenses incurred and revenues earned. As for example, payment vouchers, receipt vouchers, invoices, stamped paid, purchase orders, CBS for local purchase, petty cash vouchers (receipt and paid out), goods inspection and return report or goods received a note, taking and handing over of materials.

That organization is on a strong footing or otherwise regarding its financial planning (as revealed by cash flow, income and expenditure statement and balance sheet).

That cash and accruals are properly taken care of. (cash received and spent, payments yet to be received (time lag), recorded in ledger but yet to realized due to time lag as in accrual accounting system)

That keeps the managers to know and plan according to their financial position.

To make managers know how the planned budget and actual expenditure is going.

Managers, what the net income and expenditure are?

What liabilities to pay and what the organization owes to others. (through balance sheet)

How to accommodate the surpluses and deficits?

How to meet contingencies in terms of expenditure?

How to meet the legal obligations for an external audit to take place where the money came from and how it was spent. (internal and external audit reports)

Ensures managers to plan better for the future.

When it time to get back to accounts to straighten it up. (going through an internal audit)

A good accounting system ensures better forecasting for the future. (cash flow forecast)

Systems of Accounting for NGOs

There are two types of systems of accounting in place throughout the world of NGOs. Some NGOs follows a simple system whose working area is not too much vast with little resources and the system of accounting is called "Cash System Account". Still, some NGOs follow a system more complex with multi-dimensional sectors working with multi donors and the system in place there is called "Accruals Accounting System". Accounting is basically a system of recording revenues and expenditure by following a logical system that answers the questions that how money coming in and going out, what is the proper system to record financial transactions, what the NGO owes to others and what owed by others to it, what the current and non-current assets are? These and all other questions are addressed by following a proper system of accounting so that organization assets and liabilities are properly taken care of to ensure that management keeps eye on the budget line activities within the agreed/ stipulated financial TORs.

Types of Accounting Systems:

Cash Accounting:

Characteristics of Cash Accounting:

A very basic type of accounting as money comes and money goes out.

No outstanding bills and accruals

No liabilities as cash come, deposited in the bank and withdrawn and paid out and none owes money to the organization.

Expense and expenditure are supported by documentary pieces of evidence.

Non-cash transactions are not recorded as a donation in kind and depreciation of assets. So the process in accrual accounting goes like the following:

Diagram No 41, Accounting Accruals:

Accrual Accounting — By IQBAL SHAH

Receiepts — Incurred but yet to be realized

Records are kept in committed receivable register

Time lag factor exists

Payments — Incurred but yet to be paid out

Records are kept in committed expenditure registers

2. Accruals Accounting

In accrual accounting system there is a time lag factor that records all those revenues and expenses that are promised/ contracted/ conditioned/ incurred but not actually realized yet due to time factor. Assets and liabilities are recorded when they incurred but still receipts and payment yet to be realized. As for example, an NGO bought a laptop valued Rs60000 subject to payment after one month as agreed in the contract with the supplier, so the accountant noted it down in the journal ledger, but after one month when the invoice is paid out, then accrued payment turned into actual and recorded asset register and cash inventory book. So accrual accounting records all those payment and receipts when they incurred, but not yet actually paid or received. An accountant has to keep the following account books updated with all the supporting documents. See all these books/register in chapter 8 on finance procedures and formats.

Journal ledger	Stock book
Ledger	Petty cash log
Cashbook	Salary register
Bank or passbook	Tax deduction register
Asset register	

In cash book, two terms are used which need to be explained, as "carried forward" and "brought forward".

Carried forward

It is the amount which remained as balance in the existent month after balancing receipts and payments. As for example, if an organization receives Rs 7000 and spends $ 4000 then the revenue and expense balance will be $ 3000, and that balance is carried forward to the next month.

Brought Forward

It is a balanced amount of the previous month which is brought forward to the current month. As mentioned in the above example the balance amount of Rs 3000.

At the end of each month, a bank reconciliation statement is prepared to adjust cash book and book. A diligent accountant or finance officer has to take care of bank reconciliation statement as differences may occur due to time lag, as giving cheque and its actual cashing or bank charges missing on cash book or interests on account etc. See the diagram below.

Diagram No 42,

Bank Reconciliation Statement:

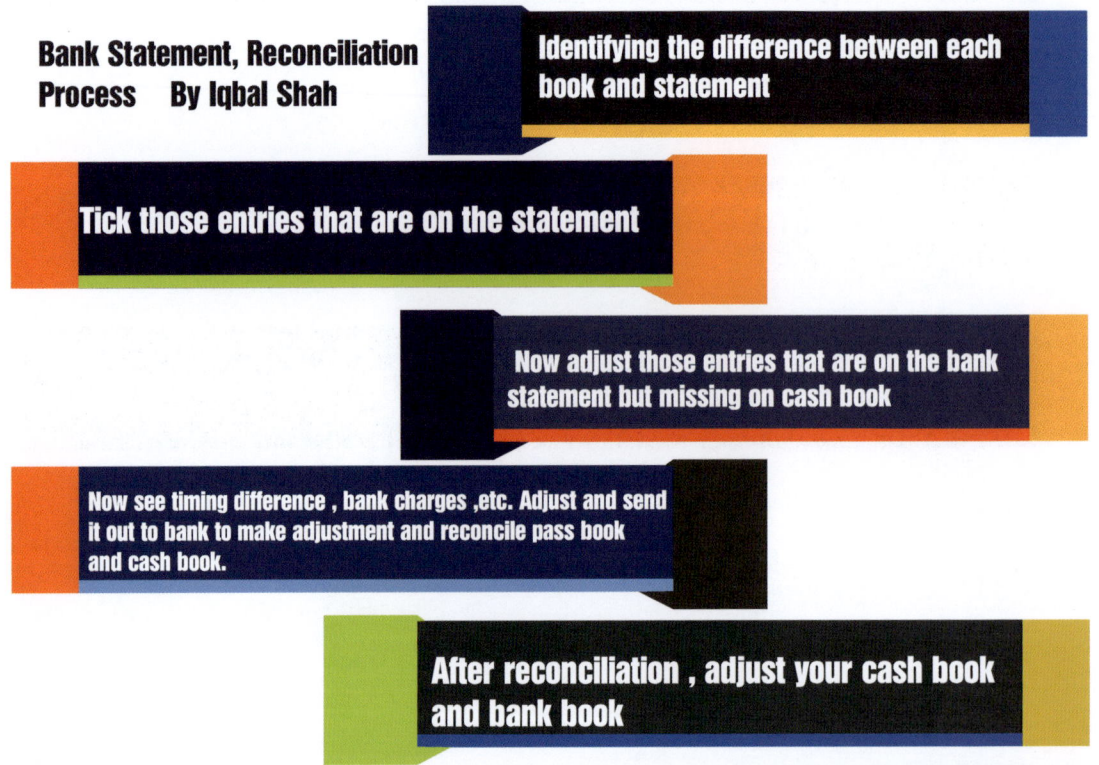

Cash Book

Date	Budget code	Description	Deposits	Withdrawals	balance
		total	total		

Balance brought forward	
Total receipts	
Total payment	
Balance carried forward	

Prepared by_____

Checked by_____

CHEQUE BOOK REGISTER (A4 SIZE PAPER IN LANDSCAPE)

CHEQUE BOOK REGISTER									
DATE	TRANSACTION TYPE	TRANSACTION#	PAYEE	PAYER	DEPOSITS	AMOUNT	RECONCILED	BALANCE	

Bank Book pass Book)

Date	Details	Debit	Credit	Balance

Employees advance salaries and loan record

	Employees advance/ salaries and loan record						
Sr.#							
Employee name							
Designation							
Department							
Loan taken							
Purpose of Loan							
Monthly Repayment							
Repayment Period							
Repay start date/month							
Advance salary							
Monthly Repayment							
Repayment Period							
Loan Repayment start							
Date / month							
ADV salary Repayment							
start date/month							
Loan Deduction							
Advance salary							
Deduction							
Total Deduction							
Loan Balance							
ADV salary Balance							
Total Balance							
Remarks							

Payroll Sheet (Excel sheet)t

Company Name _____ Department _____ Location _____

							Sr.no
							Employee ID
							Employee name
							Designation
							Bank account of employee
							Gross salary
						Working days	normal
							leave
							total
						Salary and allowances	Basic
							Utilities
							HRA
							medical
							reimbursement
							Total
						Deduction	tax
							Provident fund
							advance
							loan
							Other
							Total
							Net salary payable

Prepared by _____

Checked by _____

Verified by _____

Approved by _____

Cheque book Register/withdrawa and Deposit Record (A 4 landscape)

Date	Transaction Type	Transaction No	Payer/ payee	Category	Note	Withdrawal/ Credit	Deposit Debit	Balance

Petty Cash Vouchers

Account	Description	Amount
	Total Cash Amount Rs	

Voucher #: _____ **Received by** _____

Authorized by: _____

Pay slip

Organization name logo and address go here

Employee Signature: _____

Payment no.	Date	Amount	
PAY	31 March 2019	USD$	
Paid to:			
	Mr./Miss/Mrs.		
	Passport/Employee Id No:		
Description			
Salary per month	PKRs.00		
Shortage	PKRs.		
Advance payment	PKRs.		
Loan deduction	PKRs.		
Adv deduction	PKRs.		
Total amount payable	PKRs.		

Salary Certificate

Employee Name		Employee ID	
Department		Designation	
Salary Details			
Gross salary			
Tax deduction			
Allowance cumulative			
Net Pay			

We are awarding this pay certificate to the above mentioned employee who has worked in our organization on post of Project Manager.

Prepared by Finance Department: _____ Checked by HRM: _____

Petty Cash Custodian Certificate

OCO No: --------------------
---- Petty Cash Limit: ----------

Cash On Hand: ---------------------------- Date: -----------------
I. -------------- Finance Officer/ Administrator, I hereby declare that I accept the responsibilit as the CUSTODIAN of petty cash and hereafter will handle it with due diligence and care and its security thereof and will use it as mandated.
I agree and will follow all the rule regulations relating to petty cash handling and security. I personally hold myself responsible for any act of omission or commission in any disregard to this agreement. I will use petty cash as per policy given to me and will ensure that petty cash box is ready to be used as per policy, reimbursed and any spending gets account for.

-------- Signature of Petty Cash Custodian: _____
All concerned are intimated through this official letter

Chief Executive officer	Custodianship assigned by
Name ---------------- Signature ---------------- Date ------------	Name ---------------- Signature ---------------- Date ------------

Petty Cash Request:

Petty Cash Amount: ------------------

Requested petty Cash: ----------------   - Date: ----------------

Request Made by: -----------------   Custodian: ----------------

Needed
For:

--------------------   ----------------------

Charge to Account: Account No:

Approval:

Approved by: ---------------------   Received by: --------------

Petty Cash Reimbursement Request

Note: Reimbursements from petty cash cannot exceed (as per organization cash box policy. Write amount here)

Petty Cash Receipt

Date: _____ No: _____

Date		Department	
Amount Reimbursed		Custodian	
Expenses incurred			
S. No: Price	Item Description:	Units	
Charge to account		Approved By	
Authorized Signature			
Approved Amount		Received By	
Authorized Signature			

Petty Cash Receipt

Date: _____ No: _____

Amount PKRs	
Description	
Charged to	
Received by	
Approved by	

Petty Cash Journal

Petty cash flow and audit report
From _____ to _____ Cash in box:_____

Date	PV No	Description	Total Receipts	Total	Balance

Internal Audit No: _____
Internal auditor: _____
Signature: _____

Remarks:

Total cash on hand	
Reimbursed Amount	
Cash brought forward	
Custodian Signature	

Petty Cash Reconciliation

Petty cash _____
Cash on Hand: _____ Date: _____
Cash: _____

RECEIPTS

Date	Account Code	Receipts	Amount Spent

Salary advances register (a4 landscape) or excel sheet

SALARY ADVANCES REGISTER

Office: Month: Year:

DATE	NAME	DESIGNATION	DEPARTMENT	ADVANCE AMOUNT	Payment SCHEDULE	INSTALMENTS	DUCTION DATE / MONTH	DEDUCTED AMOUNT

Prepared By: Date:

Checked By: Date:

A Practical Guide to NGO and Project Management

Advance Salary Request Form

Dear Sir/Madam				
!_____ as permanent employee of is requesting your good self for advance salary for and deductions be made from Monthly salary as per organization Policy.				
Employee's Details:				
Employee ID	Department		S.S No	P.F Deduction
Joining Date			Amount Advance requested	
Supporting documents				
Signature	Head of Finance Signature			
Supervisor				
Approved by:	Rejected:			
Deductions will be made according to the following formula				
Monthly installment	Total installments			
Signature HR Manager	Signature Employee			
Sanctioned by:				

Loan Control Register

Department of finance

LOAN REGISTER - MONTHLY Control Sheet

Month	Year

Date	NAME OF EMPLOYEE	DEPARTMENT	DESIGNATION	Loans Issued	Loan repayments	BALANCE OUTSTANDING

Remark N:

Prepared By: Date:

Checked By: Date:

Standing Order for Staff Salaries

To
The manager _____
Address _____

I hereby authorize the organization the sum of USD $_____ from organization's account in favour of _____ as Staff Salaries due on29th of every month . The facility shall continue until the organization gets further notice in written from me of its termination.

Organization bank detail

Bank name _____   Address _____

Account No _____   Name _____

Account name _____   Sort Code _____

Pay to:_____

Name:_____   Account No:_____

Bank name   Sort code

Signature: _____   Date: _____

Standing Order for Office Rent

To
The manager
Address_____

I hereby authorize the organization the sum of PK Rs from organization's account in favour of as office rent due on 29th of every month . The facility shall continue until the organization gets further notice in written from me of its termination.

Organization bank detail

Bank name :_____ Address_____

Account No:_____ Account Title:_____

Sort Code:_____

Pay to:

Bank Name:_____ Account No:_____

Account holder:_____ Sort code:_____

Signature:_____ Date:_____

Standing Order for Staff Salaries

To
The manager _____
Address _____

I hereby authorize the organization the sum of USD $_____ from organization's account in favour of _____ as Staff Salaries due on 29th of every month . The facility shall continue until the organization gets further notice in written from me of its termination.

Organization bank detail

Bank name _____   Address _____

Account No _____   Name _____

Account name _____   Sort Code _____

Pay to:_____

Name:_____   Account No:_____

Bank name   Sort code

Signature: _____   Date: _____

General ledger

Month _____
General ledger Number _____

DATE	Amount Debited	Account Number	Amount	Account Credited	Account Number	Amount

Dr .... Cr

Fuel voucher (a4 size paper landscape)

SR.#	Requested by/ Driver	Vehicle No	Liters Requested	Liters filled	Fuel Type	KM Reading	Fuel Attendants Name	Authorized by	Signature

Fuel Voucher

Authorized by _____   Approved by:_____

Date	
Requested By (Driver name)	
Vehicle No	
Requestors Signature (Driver)	
Liters Requested	
Km Reading	
Fuel Type	
Fuel Attendant's Name	
Liters Filled	
Authorized by (Signature)	

Cheque Book Dispatch Register (A4 Landscape)

Voucher Ref	Cheque No	Date	Particular of Payee	Amount US$/Pak Rs	Mode of Dispatch	Date of Dispatch

Prepared by —————— Checked by ——————

Cash Disbursements Journal (A 4 Landscape or excel sheet)
Month _____
General Ledger Number _____

Date	cheque#	Payee	Account Credited	Account #	Cash	Discount	Other	Account debited	Account #	Amount payable	Other

A Practical Guide to NGO and Project Management

Payment Voucher

PV No:_____

Amount	Date	
Method of Payment		
Cash	By Cheque	Cheque
To:		
The Sum of:_____		
From: Reforgenonprofit:_____	To: Payee Name and Address	

Prepared by:_____ Checked by: _____ Approved by:_____

Salary Receipt

Salary Receipt

Salary receipt for the month of _____

Employee Name	Designation	Department	ID/passport	Joining Date	Gross Salary	Employee's signature

Prepared by _____ Checked by _____ Approved by _____

Pay Slip

Organization and Logo				
Address:				
		PAY SLIP		
Name of the Employee			**Days in the Month**	
Employee Code			**Worked Days**	
Month			**Date of Joining**	
Designation			**Leaves Taken**	
Department				
Particulars		**Amount Rs.**		**Amount PK Rs.**
	Gross	Payable		
Basic Salary				
HRA				
Transport Allowance				
Others				
Total			**Total Deductions :**	
Prepared By	Chief Executive Signature:		**Employee Signature**	

Bank Statement Reconciliation

BANK RECONCILIATION FORM

Department of finance		Currency		Month:	
Bank Statement Date:		Balance on bank statement		Bank Statement Sheet Number	
				Amount	
Less payments in accounts, not on statement (e.g. un-presented cheques)					
	Deduction	Total			
Less receipts on statements not in accounts (e.g. income received by bank)					
	Deduction	Total			
Plus payments on statements not in accounts (e.g. bank charges)					
	Addition	Total			
Adjusted balance on the bank statement:		Balance on bankbook:			
Prepared by:		Date:			

Bank Reconciliation Statement

Month and year _____

To the Manager,
Name of the Bank _____

Bank Account No _____

Branch of the Bank _____

Location of the Bank _____

Balance as per bank statement: $:

Attach bank statement

Add

Un-credited/ un-cleared cheque

Date	Cheque No	Particular	Amount

Less
Un-presented cheques
Balance as per bank Book: $:_____

Date	Cheque No	Particular	Amount

Prepared by _____ Checked by _____ Approved by: _____

Remarks _____

Cheque (Check) Book Register

CHEQUE BOOK REGISTER							
DATE	TRANSACTION TYPE	TRANSACTION#	PAYEE	PAYER	DEPOSITS AMOUNT	RECONCILED	BALANCE

Credit usage Log/Register

Credit Card Name			Enter payments as negative amounts		
Date	Description	Amount	Merchant name	Transaction fees	Balance (does not include interest)
	Book		Amazon		US$ 200.00

By Iqbal Shah

Fixed Assets Record

Fixed Asset Record With Depreciation

Date	Asset Name	Asset Class	Description	Physical location	Asset No.	Serial No.	Acquisition Cost	Description Method	Useful Life (Year)	Salvage value	Previous Description	First Year %	Description This period
Total													

155 By Iqbal Shah

Petty Cash Transaction Register

Petty Cash Transaction Register						
Cash Amount	Cheque Amount	Cheque Number	Payee	Purpose/Description	Deposit	Balance
				initial deposit as deposit		USD $

Bank Statement Reconciliation

Prepared by :_____ Cheeked by:_____ Approved by;_____

Bank Reconciliation Statement For March 2019		
Cash Book Balance	03/03/19	
Receipts		
Payments		
Cash Book Balance		
Balance as per bank statement		
Less outstanding cheques		
Balance as per Cash Book 31/03/2019		

Balance Sheet

ASSETS	AMOUNT
Current Assets:	
Cash in hand	
Cash in bank	
Accounts receivable (net)	
Accrual payment	
Vehicle insurance premium paid	
Vehicles	
Taxes paid	
bought	
Equipment bought	
Office equipment and Fixture	
Computer	
Total current assets	
Property, Plant, and Equipment:	
Land	
Buildings	
Machinery and equipment	
Equipment	
Less accumulated depreciation	
liabilities	
Account payable	
Payroll_ , taxes wages	
I Estimated income tax	
Total current liabilities	
Long term debt	
Total liabilities	

A Practical Guide to NGO and Project Management

Cash Flow Statement

Fiscal Year 2019— 2020

	June	July	August	September	October	November	December	January	February	March	April	May
Cash on hand												
Cash Receipts												
Total cash Receipts												
Available cash Total												
Cash Paid out												
Purchases												
Purchases (specify)												
Payroll												
Payroll Taxes												
Taxes other												
Repair/maintenance												
Office supply												
Flyers												
Office Rent												
Vehicle maintenance												
Telephone bills												
Utilities												
Insurance												
Other expenses												
Sub -total												
Total paid out												
Cash at month end												
Non cash flow												
Account payable												
Depreciation												

By Iqbal Shah

Budget Monitoring report

Financial report		Project: Bonded Lab our			1st Oct 2019 to March 2020	
Code	Budget Items	Total Budget Grant	Actual to Oct	Variance spent	% budget variance	Remarks
Administration Personnel						
Project manager						
Project Coordinator						
Social Organizers						
Supporting Staff						
Sub- Total						
Office Running Cost						
Utilities						
Telephone- emails- Postages						
Rent						
Equipment repair /maintenance						
Fuel						
Vehicle Repair						
Office supply						
Bank charges						
Sub- Total						
Total Administration Cost						
Assets cost						
Desk / Chairs/ tables						
Computer/ laptop						
Total capital Cost						
Programme Running Cost						
Training						
Field visits						
Monitoring and Documentation						
Total programme cost						
Grand Total						

CREDIT MEMO

DATE_____

BILL FROM:			BILL TO:		
I enclose copies of our invoice as under-mentioned numbers which is currently overdue for payment.					
Invoice No	Item/services	Quantity	Description	Price	Total

Cheque book Register/withdrawal and Deposit Record

Date	Transaction Type	Transaction #	Payer/Payee	Category	Note	Withdrawal/Credit	Deposit Debit	Balance

NOTICE OF DISHONORED CHECK

Date : _____/_____/_____

To : _____

Your check in the amount of Rs_____, tendered to us on 2019 _, has been dishonored by your bank.

Unless we receive bona fide reasons for the dishonored cheque funds for said amount within _____ days of receipt of this notice, otherwise we will be leaving with no other option but to proceed against you with legal action.

Very truly,

_____

Depreciation method
Depreciation Schedule
Understanding Depreciation Method

A laptop worth Pak Rs---------------- was bought by CDAAN, now the wear and tear and its usefulness for the three years will depreciated with 25% cut a year for three. The formula will be as follows:

Year	Depreciation % calculation	net value remained
Year 1	Rs10,000/100X25=2,500	Rs7,500
Year 2	Rs7,500/100X25=1,875	Rs5625
Year 3	Rs5625/100X25=1.406.25	Rs4218.75

Accounts receivable ledger

Company	Accounts receivable ledger	
Client name		Client Ref: # limitation on credit

REF

DATE	INVOICE #	REFERENCE	CHARGES	CREDITS	BALANCE

Aging of Accounts Payable

Reporting Period

From _____   To _____

Date	Invoice #	Account	Account #	Description	Amount			
					30 Days	60 Days	90+ Days	Total

Income and Expenditure account
Year 2019 to 2020

Income			
Donors			
Donation And Fundraising			
Training			
Bank interests			
Total Income			
Expenditure			
Personnel Cost			
Training expenses			
Vehicle costs of running			
Assets Description			
Administrative cost			
External audit			
Board meeting			
Flyers			
Postage and stationary			
Rent and Utilities			
Insurances			
Repair and maintenance			
Telephone and Fax			
Assets bought			
Total Expenditure			

A Practical Guide to NGO and Project Management

Project Budget worksheet

S #	Line Items	Funding Sources			Project Duration	Amount in Rupees
		Own Contributions	Requested from Donor	Other sources (provide names)	No. of Months/ Years (Unit cost)	
1	**Overhead Costs:**					
1.1	Equipment					
1.2	Administration/ logistical					
1.3	Project staff/ personnel					
1.4	Any other costs					
	Sub-Total 1					
2	**Programme Costs:**					
2.1	Activities					
2.2	Services					
2.3	Follow up					
2.4	Any other costs					
	Sub-Total 2					
3	**Own Contribution:**					
3.1	Cash – provide details					
3.2	In–kind– provide details					
3.3	Any other costs					
	Sub-Total 3					

CHAPTER FIVE:

Non-profit / NGO Administration:

Administration is that part of management system in place to mentor, facilitate and provide back up to all other staffs. The first and foremost duty of administration is to ensure that policies are written in employees' manual and office circular are disbursed and adhered to and new policies from management are to be interpreted and makes sure to reach them on time.

Responsibilities of Administration Department:

The role it plays is very important for creating conditions where all staffs have peace of mind regarding their functions and duties, facilitating different department in their working conditions, safeguarding office assets, maintaining security, distributing circulars from the side of management pertaining to amendment in the policy or new policies that are to be followed regarding certain policy procedures. Following are the procedures and formats that the administration department follows to create better working conditions whereby a staff member performs his/her duties in peaceful, collaborative manners according to some set parameters.

In order to make the work smooth, collaborative on achieving project objectives, the department of administration has to follow these procedures for a better work environment to create and ensure staff compliance with them.

Non-profit/ NGO Standard operating procedures

Standard Operating Procedures come as follow:

Employee Daily Attendance Sheet

Date: _____ / _____ / _____

Name	Sing in	Sign out	Signature	Supervisor Signature

A Practical Guide to NGO and Project Management

Employee duty schedule

Employee day/ night schedule

DATE	TIMING		Employee Name	1	2	3	4	5	6	7
	8 AM TO 4 PM	SAT								
		SUN								
		MON								
		TUE								
		WED								
		THU								
		FRI								
		TOTAL								
			Employee Name	1	2	3	4	5	6	7
	4 PM TO 12 AM NIGHT	SAT								
		SUN								
		MON								
		TUE								
		WED								
		THU								
		FRI								
		TOTAL								
			Employee Name	1	2	3	4	5	6	7
	12AM NIGHT TO 8AM MORNING	SAT								
		SUN								
		MON								
		TUE								
		WED								
		THU								
		FRI								
		TOTAL								

A Practical Guide to NGO and Project Management

Overtime Form (Excel Sheet)

Daily Overtime sheet

From _____ To _____

Sr.#	Employee Name	Designation	Department	Authorized by	Overtime		Total Hours/days	Remarks
					From	To		

Leave Application

Leave Information					
Employee Name					
Employee ID:			Department:		
Project Manager:					
Type of Absence Requested:					
Sick		Vacation		Bereavement	Time Off Without Pay
Paternity leave				Maternity	Other
Dates of Absence: From:		To:			
Reason for Leave:					
Employee Signature		Date			
Project Manager's Approval					
		Approved			
		Rejected			
Comments:					
Manager Signature			Date		

Copy to: 1 Finance Department. 2. HR department

A Practical Guide to NGO and Project Management

Absence Report

Absence Report
Employee details:
 Name:_____ Department:_____

Reported by:_____ Project Manager:_____

Leave:_____Auhoized:_____ Un-authorized____

Reasons for absence:_____
_____

Employee Signature:_____

forwarded and record kept:

HR Department:_____ finance Department:_____

Personnel records:

Prepared:_____ Checked by:_____

Organization· · · · · · Employee Leave Record

Employee Leave Record							
SR.#							
EPM.ID							
NAME							
FATHER NAME							
DEPARTMENT							
DESIGNATION							
EARNED LEAVE	LEAVE						
CASUAL LEAVE							
SICK LEAVE							
EARNED LEAVE	TOTAL LEAVE AVAILED						
CASUAL LEAVE							
SICK LEAVE							
LEAVE WITHOUT PAY							
EARNED LEAVE	BALANCE LEAVE						
CASUAL LEAVE							

By Iqbal Shah

A Practical Guide to NGO and Project Management

Petty cash Request

Petty Cash Amount: ----------------------------------

Requested petty Cash: ---------------------------- Date: ------------------

Request Made by: ---------------------------- Custodian: ----------------

Needed

For:

Charge to Account: Account No:

Approval:

Approved by: --

Received by: ------------------------------------

Petty Cash Reimbursement Request

Note: Reimbursements from petty cash cannot exceed (as per organization cash box policy. Write amount here)

Petty Cash Receipt

Date: _____ No: _____

Date		Department	
Amount Reimbursed		Custodian	
Expenses incurred			
S. No: Price	Item Description:	Units	
Charge to account		Approved By	
Authorized Signature			
Approved Amount		Received By	
Authorized Signature			

Petty Cash Receipt

Date: _____ No: _____

	Amount PKRs
Description	
Charged to	
Received by	
Approved by	

172   By Iqbal Shah

Petty Cash Reconciliation

Petty cash _____
Cash on Hand: _____ **Date:** _____
Cash: _____

RECEIPTS

Date	Account Code	Receipts	Amount Spent

Payment Voucher

PV # _____

For the Receiver Record

Prepared by _____ **Checked by:** _____
Approved by: _____

Amount:		Date:	
	Method of Payment		
By Cash:	By Cheque:		Cheque # :
	From:		
	To:		
The sum of:		Payee:	
Checked and recorded by Finance Officer			
Receiver	Paid By:		Approved By:
Payment Voucher		Pv No: _____	
Amount:	Date:		
	Method of Payment		
Cash:	By Cheque:		Cheque # :
To:			
The Sum of:			
From:		To: Payee Name and Address	

Petty Cash Custodian Certificate

OCO No: --------------------
---- Petty Cash Limit: ----------

Cash On Hand: --------------------------- Date: -----------------
I. -------------- Finance Officer/ Administrator, I hereby declare that I accept the responsibility as the CUSTODIAN of petty cash and hereafter will handle it with due diligence and care and its security thereof and will use it as mandated.

I agree and will follow all the rule regulations relating to petty cash handling and security. I personally hold myself responsible for any act of omission or commission in any disregard to this agreement. I will use petty cash as per policy given to me and will ensure that petty cash box is ready to be used as per policy, reimbursed and any spending gets account for.

-------- Signature of Petty Cash Custodian
All concerned are intimated through this official letter

Chief Executive officer	Custodianship assigned by
Name ---------------- Signature ---------------- Date -------------	Name ---------------- Signature ---------------- Date -------------

A Practical Guide to NGO and Project Management

Petty Cash Journal

Petty cash flow and audit report
From _____ to _____ Cash in box _____

Date	PV No	Description	Total Receipts	Total	Balance

Internal Audit No: _____
Internal auditor: _____
Signature: _____

Remarks: _____
_____
_____
_____

Total cash on hand	
Reimbursed Amount	
Cash brought forward	
Custodian Signature	

Trucker's Log Book (excel sheet)

Week Ending: ___/___/_____

Drivers Name: _____

Goods/Items ID _____

Starting Odometer Reading: _____ Ending Odometer Reading: _____

Warehouse Incharge Remarks: _____
_____
_____

_____   _____
Warehouse incharge Signature: Logistician

By Iqbal Shah

A Practical Guide to NGO and Project Management

Vehicle log Book for the driver

Name of _____ employee No _____ log for the month _____

Vehicle type _____ vehicle no _____

vehicle registration no _____

Date the journey/ time		Time		Odometer reading		KM travelled	Purpose of the journey	Date of entry	Name of the driver	Name of the person making entry	Signature of person making entry
Began	Ended	Start	Ended	Start	Finish						

By Iqbal Shah

Travel Authorization form

Travel Authorization Form

Employee's Details

Employee Name: _____ Employee ID: _____

Department: _____ Supervisor: _____

Travel Details:

Travel from: _____ Travel to: _____

Mode of transportation: _____

Travel Reimbursement: _____

Reimbursement Adv.: _____ Approved by: _____

Employee's certification: I hereby declare that upon my travel mission completion, all vouchers regarding expense will be submitted to finance department.

Employee's Signature: _____

Approving Authority: _____

Employee supervisor: _____ CEO Approval: _____

Signature: _____ Date: _____

Signature: _____ Date: _____

A Practical Guide to NGO and Project Management

Vehicle Schedule of Field Trips

Vehicle Registration No	Purpose of Visit	Person incharge	Driver Name	Week
				Monday
				Tuesday
				Wednesday
				Thursday
				Friday
				Saturday
Note				

Equipment Repair Form

Date_____ ERR No:_____

Requisitioner		Department	
Asset Description			
Asset type	Asset No	Issued to	Date of Issue
Repair needed			
Parts needed	Kind of parts		Vendor

The Requisitioner must sign this form and return it to the custodian of assets and who must

approve of from CEO.

Requisitioner name:_____ Custodian of assets:_____

Checked by inventory Controller:_____

Approved by CEO:_____

Note: The form should be signed by the requesting staff and countersigned by the custodian of assets and

approved by the CEO

Vehicle repair log

Driver Name		Year	
License No		Make	
Driver ID		Model	
Passport No		Vehicle ID No	
National Identity No		Registration No	
		Vehicle Type	

S #	Date	Description	Workshop name	Contact #	Mechanic Name	Labour cost	Parts	Parts cost	Vender name	Total cost
								Total repair expense		

Checked by: _____ **Approved by:** _____

Equipment sign in and sign out Sheet

SR.#	Purpose	Out date	Time	Asset No	Custodian	Department	In Date	Time in	Signature

A Practical Guide to NGO and Project Management

Vehicle Accident Report

Vehicle Accident Report	Logistics unit:_____
	Administration _____
	Date:_____
Vehicle No:_____	User's Name:_____
Department:_____	

Description of Accident

Date_____ and time:_____

Location_____

Damage to Vehicle:_____

Injury (If Any):_____

Detail Description:_____

Vehicle User's Signature:_____

logistics / administration:_____

Verification And Comments   _____

Vehicle accident ---------------continued page 2

Vehicle current location:_____

Eyes witnesses_____

Witness 1:_____ Address_____ Phone

No:_____

Witness 2: _____ Witness 3: _____

Police Report if any:_____

Charges: 1:_____ 2 :_____ 3:_____

Type of accident:_____

Information:

Police informed: Yes or No   Relative of dead or injured informed: Yes or No

Insurance company informed: Yes or No

Note : Police report . accident diagram and insurance company report must be attached with this report for follow up.

By Iqbal Shah

Accident/ incident follow up sheet

Accident / incident reference no:_____

Vehicle registration no : _____

Attachment to be received within specified date.

1. Accident/ incident report form(2 copies)
2. Trip/ mission authority form
3. Vehicle's operator license
4. Pictures of vehicle
5. Police case report

Officer responsible for follow up

Name: _____

Date of report: _____

Checklist on the progress of follow up

Date	Follow up	progress
	Attachment received	
	Police informed	
	Insurance company notified	
	Condition and location of injured	
	Relatives of injured/ dead notified	
	Contact with other party made	
	Contact with eye witnesses	
	Internal people notified	
	Distribution of documents copies	
	Safe keeping of vehicle keys	
	C cancellation of cards	
	Arrangement for vehicle repair	
	Vehicle operator follow up/ training	
	Conclusion	
Other remarks:		

A Practical Guide to NGO and Project Management

Purchase Order

Purchase order No: _____
Attention: _____ **Date:** _____
Dear Supplier:
Address: _____
As agreed per quotation, you are requested to supply the following items to our Procurement/administration department.
Note: Any damage items will be returned with a GIRN.

Items	Description	Unit	Total Units	Unit price	Total price
			Total units		
			Total Price		

Prepared by: _____ **Checked by:** _____

Approved by: _____

Travel Expense Report

Employee's Name: _____ **Date Submitted:** _____
Submitted to: _____
Details of items
Date   Voucher #   Description   Amount

Remarks by finance officer:_____

Approved by: _____ **Authorized by :** _____

Authorized Signature: _____

By Iqbal Shah

A Practical Guide to NGO and Project Management

Purchase Order

Purchase Order	Name of Supplier	Delivery Date	Items description	Quantity			GRN		Remarks
				Ordered	Delivered	Balance	Date	No	

Prepared by_____   Reviewed by_____

Purchase Order

Purchase order No: _____
Attention: _____   Date: _____
Dear Supplier:
Address: _____
As agreed per quotation, you are requested to supply the following items to our Procurement/administration department.
Note: Any damage items will be returned with a GIRN.

Items	Description	Unit	Total Units	Unit price	Total price
			Total units		
			Total Price		

Prepared by: _____   Checked by: _____

Approved by: _____

By Iqbal Shah

A Practical Guide to NGO and Project Management

Purchases stock book

Sr #	PO#	PV#	Invoice #	Supplier	Delivery Date	Items description	Quantity			GRN		Issue office	Remarks
							Requisitioned	Delivered	Balance	Date	No		

Order Acceptance Notice

Attention:_____ Date:_____

We are submitting this notice to 'verify our acceptance of the following goods:

Date	P.O #	Currency ($)	Insurance #	Shipment No

We find these goods to be acceptable, in good condition, free of damage

or defect, and in accordance to our order.

We accept this shipment of' goods.

Thank you,

Sincerely,

(Authority Signature):_____

Quotation Records (excel Sheet)

Date	Purchase order #	Quantity	List price	Net price	Discounts	Weigh	Unit	Total	Vendor	Remarks

Comparative bid statement analysis

Selection Criteria	Supplier 1	Supplier 2	Supplier 3
Quality			
Quantity			
Cost effective			
Supplier's efficiency			
Packaging quality			
Mode of transportation			
Transportation cost			
Market credibility			
Tax status			
After sale service			
Warranty			
Change of items policy			
Payment conditions			
Recommended supplier:			
Criteria for recommendations			

Prepared by _____ Checked by:_____

Supply Requisition slip

Requisition: _____							
Requisitioner: _____							
Approved By: _____							
Description	Needed by	Department	Unit	Total units	unit price	Total price	Remarks
						Total	

Requisition of parts for the maintenance and repair of vehicle

Name driver	Driver ID No	Registration No	Vehicle No	Vehicle Type	Model	Make

Part name	Part no	Price	Company make	Vendor	Workshop Contact	Mechanic name
Total Price						
Remarks						

Driver Signature -------------------------Logistic Officer Signature ---------------------

CEO Signature --

Request for Quotation

From: _____Organization name and Address

We are requesting quotations from reputable firms to provide net rate for the following items.

Your Quotations must reach the undersigned within 8 days of this advertisement.

Successful firm will be notified on:_____

Date:_____ QR No:_____

S#:	Items	Description	Amount
Total			
Supplier Name and Address:			

Administrative Officer:_____ Date:_____

Supply inward record

Transporter name:_____

Destination:_____

Means of transport:_____

Date of dispatch:_____

Dispatch No:_____

Date of arrival:_

Description	Quantity	Weight	Units	Remarks
Quantity of packages		Total weight in KGs		

Name, signature of recipient: place and date:_____

Remarks (report any discrepancy, damage or shortage):_____

Reason for return or issue: _____

A Practical Guide to NGO and Project Management

ASSETS INVIENTORY/ ASSETS RECORD REGISTER (Excel Sheet)

Items description			Current location			Purchase information	Quality and value	Items details
S#								
Items								
Description								
			Current location					
			Deptt					
			Room#					
			Issued to					
						Date purchased		

By Iqbal Shah

A Practical Guide to NGO and Project Management

Asset Register (A4 Landscape paper)

Month _____ Year _____

Asset	Description	Current location	Issued to	Purchase date	Purchase price	Currency	Accounts Code	Accounts Ref((PV #)	Last Verified date	Notes

Prepared by: Date: _____

Checked by Date _____

Date last modified: _____

By Iqbal Shah

A Practical Guide to NGO and Project Management

Delivery Receipt Form

Supplier: Receipt
No: Invoice #:
Supplier's
address:
Date

Dear,

I hereby acknowledge receipt of the Following in perfect condition and as per the set conditions of our supply contract:

Description	Quantity Delivered	Weight	units	P O #

Received by :_____

Checked by:_____

By Iqbal Shah

PaymentVoucher

PV No: _____

Amount	Date	
Method of Payment		
Cash	By Cheque	Cheque
To:		
The Sum of:_____		
From: Reforgenonprofit:____		To: Payee Name and Address

Prepared by: _____ Checked by: _____ Approved by: _____

Confirmation of goods (Materials) Received

Name of the company:_____

Date	Quantity	Description	Shipment origin	Shipment to	Shipment received	Signature:
				Grand Total		

Authorized by:_____

Guest book (Visitor book)

Date	Guest Name	Guest ID	Purpose of Visit	From (Organization)	Phone/ cell No	Sign in	Sign out	Signature

Goods Received Note

GRN No:_____   Date:_____

Supplier and purchase Information		
Supplier	Purchase Order No	Delivery No
Invoice Reference	Date Received	Mode of Delivery
Items Details		

S#	Store Code	Description	Quantity				Required date
			Needed	Available	Last supply	To be purchased	

Prepared by: _____   Checked by: _____

Approved by:—————————————————

A Practical Guide to NGO and Project Management

Goods Inspection and Return Report (GIRN)

Date: _____   GIR NO: _____

Goods Purchase and Delivery Report	
Purchased order reference	
Department/ Location	
Supplier's Name and phone#	
Supplier's Address	
Date of Delivery	
Delivery note reference	
Place of Delivery	
Description of goods	
Quantity	
Warranty (if any)	

Goods Receipt and Inspection Report					
We hereby certify that all goods have been received and inspected by us and we have found that all the good are in usable condition and there are no shortage and damages and/ or noted below.					
Authorized Signature		Authorized Signature		Authorized Signature	
Name		Name		Name	
Date		Date		Date	

Goods Return if any	
Goods Return Note no	
Date	
Department/ Location	
Supplier's Name and phone#	
Supplier's Address	
Date of Delivery	

Items Rejected (Details)			
Item Rejected	Quantity	Item Rejected	Quantity

By Iqbal Shah

A Practical Guide to NGO and Project Management

Handing over & Taking over of vehicle

This form specifies the official handing over and taking over of vehicle limn the Seller to the Buyer

Vehicle Details		Vehicle Regd: No	
Make			
Model			
Colour		Date of take over	
Vehicle		Time	
Year		Odometer	KM
Engine No			
Chassis No			
Buyer Details			
Name			
CNIC Number			
Contact Number			
Address			
Seller Details			
Name			
CNIC Number			
Contact Number			
Address			

The Buyer hereby acknowledges receipt and assumes all responsibilities of

all the above described vehicles from the date and time stated above.

Buyer Signature _____

Seller Signature _____

1 Witness _____   2 Witness: _____

ID _____   ID _____

By Iqbal Shah

ISSUE LOG (Excel)

Date Reported	Issue No	Issue description	Reported by	Actions proposed	Actions taken	Due Date	Priority	Status

---

Request for opening account for new employee

Date:_____ Place:_____

To

Bank Manager,

BANK NAME:_____

_____Branch.

Sub: To open a New Account in your Bank.

Respected sir,

With reference to the above subject, please open an account to our employee.

Mr._____ working as an accountant in our organization from last 6 months and he is staying in our campus.

Please do the needful and open his account in your branch.

Thanking you

Yours faithfully,

(Administrator)

A Practical Guide to NGO and Project Management

LOSS AND DAMAGE REPORT

SHIPMENT NO		DESTINATION	
DATE: DRIVER ID		VIHICLE NO: LOCATION	
DESCRIPTION	NUMBER OF UNITS	NET KG EACH	TOTAL

Nature and extent of loss, damage or misuse:_____

Who were the persons/agency having possession at the time of loss:_____

Details of circumstances under which loss/damage / misuse happened:_____

Current location and disposition of commodities:_____

What actions have been taken to effect recovery:_____

What actions have been taken to predate further losses or damages:_____

Other comments:_____

Prepared by: Date:_____

Checked by: Date:_____

Approved by: Date:_____

REGISTER OF LETTER DISPATCHED (A4 Landscape or excel sheet)

Issue Ref #	Date	Name	Designation	Place to be dispatched	Courier	Subject / Contents	File Head #	Stamps Used	Stamps Price	Remarks

Register of Letter Received (A4 landscape or Excel Sheet)

Sr.#	DATE	REFERENCE	RECEIVED FROM	SUBJECT	FILE HEAD	DISPOSAL	FOLIO#

Staff Movement Register

Date: _____

Logo / Name of the Organization: _____

Address of the Organization: _____

Staff Movement Register: _____

Location of office: _____

S#	Name	Designation	Place to be visited	Purpose of visit	Permission granted by	Time Out	Time In	Total time out	Status of visit	Remarks

Personnel emergency record

Name		Soc. Sec. No.	
Address		Telephone	
City		In Emergency Notify Relationship	
Address		Telephone	
Physician		Telephone	
Dentist		Telephone	
Medication Currently Taking		Insurance	

This form has been completed on (date): _____

Meeting Agenda/ Purpose

Meeting Agenda: - _____

Topic	Time allotted	Presenter
Issues brought forward from previous meeting		Issue status
		1 As pending
		2 In progress
		3 Postponed
		4 neglected

Decisions taken

Topics	Decision taken

Task assigned:

Topics	Notes
1	
2	
3	

Meeting minutes

Topics	Responsible person
1	
2	
3	
Decision Taken:	

Previous meeting issues

Topics1	Notes
2	
3	
3	
Previous meeting issues	
Topics /issues	Notes
1	
2	
3	
4	
Decisions taken	
Topics /issues	Decision
1	
2	
3	
4	
Tasks assigned	
Topics /issues	Tasks assigned to/ responsible person
1	
2	
3	
4	
5	

Suggestion Form

Suggestions/Request

Text here

Suggestion submitted by:_____

Date of Suggestion:_____

Suggestions Forwarded to:_____

A Practical Guide to NGO and Project Management

DRIVER'S INSPECTION REPORT
CHECK DEFECTS ONLY • • • EXPLAIN UNDER REMARKS

LOCATION/DEPARTMENT: _____ DATE: _____

VEHICLE DESCRIPTION: YEAR: _____ MAKE: _____ MODEL: _____

SERIAL NO.: _____ MILEAGE: _____

GENERAL CONDITION
- ■ Cab/Doors/Windows
- ■ Body/Doors
- ■ Oil Leak
- ■ Grease Leak
- ■ Coolant Leak
- ■ Fuel Leak
- ■ Other _____

(Identify)

ENGINE COMPARTMENT
- ■ Oil Level
- ■ Coolant Level
- ■ Other Safety Equipment
- ■ Brake connection
- ■ Coupling Chain
- ■ Springs
- ■ Crane
- ■ Coupling (king) pin

(Identify)

INTERIOR
- ■ Gauges/Warning Indicators
- ■ Windshield Wipers/Washers
- ■ Horn
- ■ Heater/Defroster
- ■ Mirrors
- ■ Steering
- ■ Clutch
- ■ Service Brakes
- ■ Parking Brake
- ■ Emergency Brakes
- ■ Caution Triangles/Flares
- ■ Fire Extinguisher
- ■ Tie Downs
- ■ Spare Fuses
- ■ Seat Belts
- ■ spindle
- ■ crankshaft

EXTERIOR
- ■ Lights
- ■ Reflectors
- ■ Suspension
- ■ Tires
- ■ Wheels/Rims/Lugs
- ■ Battery
- ■ Exhaust
- ■ Brakes
- ■ Air Filter
- ■ Spare Tire
- ■ Dents
- ■ Other Coupling
- ■ Rear-End Protection
- ■ Other

Identify)

REMARKS: _____
_____
_____
_____

REPORTING DRIVER: _____ DATE: _____
                        (Name)

REVIEWING DRIVER: _____ DATE: _____
                        (Name)

MAINTENANCE ACTION: REPAIRS MADE _____ NO REPAIRS NEEDED ■

VENDOR _____

WORK ORDER / PURCHASE ORDER NO.: _____

By Iqbal Shah

Hotel booking requisition

To

Administrator

(Name here)

Kindly make reservations as per details mentioned below

Name of the Guest		Designation	
Name of Organization		Bill payment	
Department		Rooms	
Name Of Hotel		Expenses	
Date & Time of Arrival		Date and Time of Departure	
Arriving from		Departing to	
Special Requirements (if any)			

Signature of Employee: _____ Authorized Signature:_____

Note: Employees of designation Programme Manager and above are authorized to approve the requisition including their own

Loan Application Form

Your Organization's Name

LOAN REQUEST FORM / LOAN RECORD

Request			
Terms of loan		Monthly Repayments	
Loan amount		Repayment period	
Person requesting loan			
Purpose of loan:			

Authorized by: _____ signature: _____ Date: _____

Loan received by: _____ signature: _____ Date: _____

Repayment Plan				
Date	Amount outstanding	Payment due	Balance	Payment made ?	Signature

Salary advances and loan register

S#	Employee Name	Designation	Department	Month	Loan Taken	Adv Salary	Deduction to be made		Balance	Signature employee
							Loan	Adv salary	Adv salary	

Assignment Change Request Log

Sr.#	Request Title	Request Date	Originator	Assigned To	Response Date	Status	Close Date

Log Custodian_____

Employee status form

Employee Name_____ Employee Code_____

Job title Department_____

Location_____

Status change effective from:_____

title change Current title Raised:_____

title:_____

transfer   transfer from _____

                              transfer to_____

Department change _____Current dept _____new dept_____

Salary change _____Current salary_____ Revised salary_____

Change in personal   information_____

Remarks:_____

Processing of employee status form

Initiated by_____ Checked by_____ verified by_____ approved by_____

Date _____Date _____Date _____Date_____

HUMAN RESOURCES DEPARTMENT CHECKLIST

Database updated, Department head notified_____ Director / Manager Human Resources

Personal file updated finance department informed_____   Approved by:_____

Claim for Damage

T (CARRIER):	From (Claimant)
Shipment Details	
Supplier	
Invoice NO	
Goods Demanded	
Goods Delivered	
Total damaged items	

As_____ Shipper/_____ recipient, we hereby give Notice to you. the Carrier, that the following goods received as described above were found to be damaged:

REF#	Quantity	DESCRIPTION OF ITEMS	DESCRIPTION OF DEMAGES	VALUE
			TOTA CIAIMED PK Rs	

Compensation for the above damages is hereby claimed and demanded. Such claim does not limit our rights to further claims and damages, in the event additional claims for damages are discovered on account of such delivery. All rights reserved

Claimant:_____ Authorized:_____

Signatory:_____

Employee FactSheet

Employee name		Department	
Father's name		Designation	
Salary		Contact No	
Address		Marital Status	
Date of Birth		Date of Hiring	
Bank Account No		Branch/code	
Employee dependents			
Name		Relationship	Date of birth

I authorize the reefers to give you any or all information regarding my previous employment and pertinent information they may have, personal or otherwise

An drelease all parties from any liabilities that may result from furnishing same to you, I understand that giving any information about the Organization's finances, operation and or any other information that are confidential (unless officially authorized) to anyone including press, radio, TV and other media. It is organization's policy to treat all employees a ndapplicants for employments without regard to race, religion, gender, age and handicapped. No discrimination is allowed on the above lines. I understand this policy and will adhere to it.

    I acknowledge that the Organization receives the right to amend or modify the policies contained in its policy manual at any time without prior notice. In understand that these policies are binding on me and I will adheretothem.Thesepoliciesdonotcreateany ontractual obligationbetweenthe organizationandits employees.

    I certifythattheinformationthatI declarediscorrecttothebestofmyknowledge and
    I   understand that any holding back of information shall result In my dismissal .

Signature _____

References		
Name	Address	contact
1		
2		
3		

CHAPTER SIX

Non-profit / NGO logistics

Definition of logistics: Logistics

The procurement, maintenance, distribution, and replacement of personnel and materials. -- (Webster's Dictionary)

Logistics

The science of planning, organizing and managing activities that provide goods or services. -- (MDC, Log Link / Logistics World, 1997)

Logistics embodies the effort to deliver:

the right product

in the right quantity

in the right condition

to the right place

at the right time

for the right customer

at the right cost

In the above definition, logistics is mainly defined from a business perspective involving profit. But from NGO's perspectives, logistics can be defined as thus.

"Logistics is the supportive department of NGO which facilitate the movement and deployment of personnel in the field, securing procurement, order supply to the office and ensuring the right product ordered, in the right quantity, right condition, to the right place while following logistic procedural protocols.

Logistic Management Diagram

Logistics Management By iqbal Shah

 https://reforgenonprofit.blogspot.com/

Managing the flow of material from the source to the user

Material management and physical distribution

Material management concerned with procurement, transportation and storage of raw materials

The storgae of finished products at an intermediate place

So the logistic management concerned with the flow of materials to the right place, in right and adequate quantity and ensuring quality to an end user on time

Drivers and vehicle record

Driver Name	License No	Vehicle No	Engine No	Odometer on acquisition	Chassis No	Hired on Date	End date	Health Condition	Vendor Name

Drivers and vehicle record

Driver Name	License No	Vehicle No	Engine No	Odometer on acquisition	Chassis No	Hired on Date	End date	Health Condition	Vendor Name

Vehicle Schedule of Field Trips

Vehicle Registration No	Purpose of Visit	Person incharge	Driver Name	Week
				Monday
				Tuesday
				Wednesday
				Thursday
				Friday
				Saturday
Note				

Mileage Log

Total mileage recorded						00.00		
Date	Time	Description	Purpose	From	To	Odometer		
						Start	finish	Mileage

Requisition for parts of vehicles

		Name driver				Part name			Total Price
		Driver ID No				Part no			
		Registration No				Price			
		Vehicle No				Company make		Remarks	
		Vehicle Type				Vendor			
		Model				Workshop Contact			
		Make				Mechanic name			

Driver Signature ------------------

Logistic Officer Signature ------------------

CEO Signature ------------------

Vehicle Master Maintenance Schedule

S#	Vehicle in use of	Registration #	Make	Maintenance carried out on		Maintenance due on		Remarks
				KMs	Date	KMs	Date	

Vehicle Master Maintenance Schedule — Administration

A Practical Guide to NGO and Project Management

Vehicle maintenance record

Driver	License #	Driver ID #	Last date of checking	Vehicle type	Chassis #

Year & Make	Model #	Serial #	Oil	Inspection of work completed

Date	Odometer	Lube	Tyre Size	Company

Service and expense summary

Part #	Part # and Quantity	Driver ID #	Last date of checking	Vehicle type	Chassis #

Vehicle usage summary

Start Meter	Ending Meter	Business miles	Personal miles	Accident	Services done	Vehicle condition	Repair needed	Fuel log	Fill up date	Cost

Checking summary

Oil and filter	Battery/ cables	Brake fluid	Lights and turn signals	Steering	Tyre inflation	Transmission fluid	Wiper blades fluids	Air filter	Spark plug	Smog inspection

Checking of hoses / fluids / gas cables

Checking of hoses	Coolant check/ anti freeze	Air filter replacement	Spark plug replacement	Brake checking	Remarks

Vehicle repair log

Driver Name		Year	
License No		Make	
Driver ID		Model	
Passport No		Vehicle ID No	
National Identity No		Registration No	
		Vehicle Type	

Date	Description	Workshop name	Contact #	Mechanic Name	Labour cost	Parts	Parts cost	Vender name	Total cost
							Total repair expense		

checked by: _____   Approved by: _____

By Iqbal Shah

CHAPTER SEVEN:

Non-profit / NGO warehouse management

Defining warehousing

A system that takes care of proper handling and storage of materials; inflow and outflow records, organization of storage capacity and its proper utilization, data management with proper documentation and ensures inventory control procedures and also calls for responsible management and systematic reporting procedure. So the proper storage and utilization of materials in a systematic way are called warehouse management.

Some procedures are in place to ensure proper storage and utilization of materials by following some "Standard Operating Procedures".

A warehouse is selected on the basis of its easy access, safety and security and space needed. Due care is taken to ensure that proper documentation of all arrival, issued and in-transit stocks are kept up to date.

Routine cleaning, commodities categorization, pallets usage to safeguard commodities, stacking bin card in front of the stock and updating it, separation of damaged items, routine weekly/monthly stock physical count, good quality procedures and proper documentation are procedures that are followed to ensure quantity, quality and safeguarding materials/commodities. Chapter 7 on "Warehouse SOPs" contains all procedures currently in use.

Warehouse Management Diagram No 42:

Warehouse Management System
By Iqbal Shah

- Warehouse is a place for storage of materials with a proper inflows and outflows records

- Warehouse management is a systematic way of storing and transferring of materials having a proper documentary records of inflows and outflows.

- It is systematic way of keeping materials inflows and outflows records by using some specialized software/or doing manually.

- Warehouse is selected on the basis of its easy access, space needed, location security and safety of materials.

- Proper documentation and SOPs are followed to ensure quality and quantity.

- Books /Registers are kept updated to ensure Stock in and stock out records.

- All supporting documents are taken care of to ensure inventory control system

Ware house ledger

Date of receipt	Sender Name	Delivery #	Quantity		Cumulative receipt		Date of dispatch	Delivery #	Quantity		Destination	Stack #	Losses in total	Closing balance	Signature
			Units	MT	Units	MT			Units	Units					

WAREHOUSE IN-CHARGE:

Warehouse Inward Register

Date	Item description	Drop in time	Quantity/unit received	Difference if any	Count date	Stake no in warehouse	Any losses	Stock count

Warehouse incharge		Logistic manager		Any discrepancy in stock count		Driver name	Remarks
Signature		signature		Unit	Quantity		

Warehouse Outward Register

Date	Shipper	Way bill #	Quantity unit dispatched		Difference if any	Stake # warehouse	Any losses	Closing balance	Remarks
			Quantity	Unit					

Date	Warehouse Incharge Signature	Logistic Manager Signature	Discrepancy in stock count		Dispatch destination	Arrival time/ date
			Unit	Quantity		

GRN #	On Time	Delay(If any)	Rout Taken	Mishap on the way

Consignee: _____ ; Received by: _____ Incharge: _____

227

By Iqbal Shah

Warehouse Inventory

Warehouse Inventory Sheet (A4 landscape or excel sheet)

Quantity	Items Description	Quantity			Warehouse incharge
		Stock inward	Stock outward	Balance	

Warehouse incharge:_____

A Practical Guide to NGO and Project Management

Warehouse Receiving and Issuance Log

RD NO:_____

DATE	QUANTITY		INVOICE	QUANTITY ISSUED		BILL NO	BALANCE QUANTITY		SIGNATURE
	UNITS	RECEIVED		UNITS	RECEIVED		UNITS	RECEIVED	

Supply inward record

Transporter name:_____

Destination:_____

Means of transport:_____

Date of dispatch:_____

Dispatch No:_____

Date of arrival:_____

Description	Quantity	Weight	Units	Remarks
Quantity of packages	Total weight in KGs			

Name, signature of recipient:_____ place and date:_____

Remarks (report any discrepancy, damage or shortage):_____

Reason for return or issue:_____

By Iqbal Shah

Weekly Warehouse Report

Week 1
Monday

Item Name	In Stock	Stock Outward	Balance

Tuesday

Item Name	In Stock	Stock Outward	Balance

Wednesday

Item Name	In Stock	Stock Outward	Balance

Thursday

Item Name	In Stock	Stock Outward	Balance

Stock Inventory

Warehouse Inventory Sheet (A4 landscape or excel sheet)

Quantity	ItemsDescription	Quantity			Warehouse incharge
		Stock inward	Stock outward	Balance	

Warehouse incharge:

Vehicles Spare Parts Stock Inventory

Warehouse

Address:_

Name of mechanic	Telephone no	Mobile no	Signature

Please indicate the different spare parts that are available in the garage:

Spare parts	Description	Quantity

Please indicate the different spare parts which need to be restocked:

Spare parts	Quantity to be bought	Sale price

Shipping Note Book warehouse

Shipping #	Customer Acc No	Product code	Business process network	No of pallets	Total qnty of goods	Total weight	Sign: driver	Sign: of incharge	Vehicle Reg: No

Warehouse Receiving and issuance Log Format 2

BIN CARD NO:

DATE	QUANTITY		INVOICE	QUANTITY ISSUED		BILL NO	BALANCE QUANTITY		SIGNATURE
	UNITS	RECEIVED		UNITS	RECEIVED		UNITS	RECEIVED	

Warehouse Bin Card (discrepancy)

Date	Items	Description	Receipt		Stock count	Discrepancy noted	Signature
			Unit	Quantity			

Warehouse Bin Card (discrepancy)
Warehouse Bin Card

Date	Items	Description	Receipt		Issued items		Issued to	Stock balance	Signature
			Unit	Quantity	Unit	Quantity			

Signature of warehouse In-charge:

Authority Signature:

Shipping Invoice

Invoice No
From   To
Shipping Company   organization

Items/Goods Details
Items Description   Weight   Unit   Price

                                Tax
                         Transportation
                             Charges

Shipper Detail

Name/ Title_____ Signature_____

Order acceptance Notice

Order Acceptance Notice

Attention _____ **Date** _____

We are submitting this notice to verify our acceptance of the following goods:

Date	P.O. PK Rs	Invoice#	Shipment No

We find these goods to be acceptable, in good condition, free of damage or defect, and in accordance to our order.

We accept this shipment of goods. Thank you.

Sincerely,

........................**ADMINISTRATOR**

Waybill

Company Name			From:	
			To:	
Contact person		Contact person		
Title		Title		
Telephone No		Telephone No		
Email		Email		
Items Description				

Items	Quantity	Unit Measure	Description	Package type	Package quantity	No of pallets	Total gross weight	Total gross	Company items

Claim for Shipment damage

T (CARRIER):		From (Claimant)
Shipment Details		
Supplier		
Invoice NO		
Goods Demanded		
Goods Delivered		
Total damaged items		

As_____ Shipper/_____recipient, we hereby give Notice to you. the Carrier, that
      the
following goods received as described above were found to be damaged:

REF#	Quantity	DESCRIPTION OF ITEMS	DESCRIPTION OF DEMAGES	VALUE
			TOTAL CLAIMED PK Rs	

Compensation for the above damages is hereby claimed and demanded. Such claim does not limit our rights to further claims and damages, in the event additional claims for damages are discovered on account of such delivery. All rights reserved

Claimant:_____ Authorized
Signatory:_____

Consignment Delivery Note

Company	Delivery #:_____ Date					Place	
DOCUMENTS AND SHIPMENT INSIRUCTION ONLY							
ATTENTION:							
CONSIGNMENT ADDRESS							
Invoice	PO #	Consigned to	Pieces	Weight	Place		
						Origin	Destination

Delivery notes/
Observations:_____
_____
_____
_____

Confirmation of goods (Materials) Received

(Warehouse Record)

Name of the company:_____

Date	Quantity	Description	Shipment origin	Shipment to	Shipment received Signature:
				Grand Total	

Authorized by_____

Shuttle - Driver trip log

Date	Driver Name	Total Trip	Trips cost	Cost on trips	Bill amount

Release order

Items to be released				
Items	Description	unit	total	
		Grand total		
	Insert Warehouse Details of Goods			
Warehouse name	Lot No	Goods No	R.O.No	Incharge
Logistics Unit	Driver Name	Logistic manager	Name	Signature

Approving Authority:_____

Stock Count (Excel sheet or A4 landscape)

Stock Count Report

S#	Item description	sender	Unit	Quantity per stock card	Physical quantity counted	Discrepancy

Checked By:_____ **Warehouse In-charge:**_____

Authority Signature:_____

Expected Shipments

Arrival month	Project	Shipping instructions No	Donor	Commodity	(Qty)MTN	Status	*ETA	Entry point	*ATA	Distribution Plan	Date of issue	pre-delivery Losses

*Estimated time of Arrival

*Actual Time of Arrival

CHAPTER EIGHT

Non- profit / NGO's Human Resources Management

NGOs' Human Resources Management:

NGOs mainly depend on human resources in order to implement projects.

Definition HRM:

Human:

people with skills, knowledge and abilities.

Resources:

The workforce environment and the practices and policies that affect either the people or working condition.

Management:

The overall working environment that comes out of the relationship between policies and the workforce (Employees to employees and Employer to employees).

So human resources management is a kind of systematic way to devise and practice policies that create congenial workforce environment and ensure better employees to employees and employer to employees' relationship. It ensures to have suitable staffs, creating a congenial workforce environment in order to fulfil the organization's mission. Diagram 43, 44 and 45:

HRM Diagram No 43:

Understanding Human Resources Management
by Iqbal Shah
https://reforgenonprofit.blogspot.com/

- Suitable staff, good policies procedures and practices ensure better work environment that contributes to the organization mission.
- Hiring suitable staff to ensure quality of work

Human Resources Management

- Spotting loopholes in working conditions and environment and rectify them timely. (as training of employees, status changing, promotion and demotion)
- creating congenial work force environment by practicing policies and following certain procedures to ensure quality of work

A Practical Guide to NGO and Project Management

NGO Human Resources Management
From hiring to firing (process):

Diagram No 46:

From Hiring to Firing   By Iqbal Shah

Staffs Hiring/ Grading /Salary benefits determining	Probation period and joining
Staffs Requisitioning	Induction and joining Reports Employee Fact Sheet Prepararation
Preparing Job Description	Preparing Employee Mannual
Getting approval and Job Advertisement	probation evaluation
Cvs sorting and short listing	Job performance appraisal
Calling candidates for test	Training need assessment
Declaring suucessful candidates and contract signing	Staffs Hiring/(Charge sheeting/ reprimand /dismissal and termination)

A Practical Guide to NGO and Project Management

MAN POWER REQUEST FORM

Job Title	Date:_____ Needed:_____ From:_____ to:_____ Education and qualification:_____ Requirement:_____ Ex pereience requirement:_____ Other special skills requirements:_____

If replacement, complete the following :

Employee to be replaced: _____ Job: _____

DATE SEPARATED: _____

REASON FOR SEPARATION: _____

JUSTIFICATION FOR INCREASE IN THE STAFF: _____

IS THERE A PROVISION FOR THE POST IN THE BUDGET YES ____ NO: _____

EXPLAIN WHY IT IS NOT POSSIBLE TO AVOID THIS INCREASE BY OFFICE REARRANGEMENT)'

INITIATED BY: _____ AUTHORIZED BY: _____ APPROVED BY: _____

HEAD OF DEPARTMENT: _____ HRM : _____ CEO: _____

DATE.   DATE   DATE

By Iqbal Shah

Job Description Form

Job Title		Department	
Category		Location	
Job Specification		Open	
Job requirements			
Experience Needed		Skill Needed	
Languages		Applications		Through email

Job Description:
List job responsibilities
1
2
3
4
5
List education and preferred skills needed
Education_____
HR Manager:
Approved by CEO:

Job advertisement

Dear Sir,

Regarding our new recruitment in the administrative department, we planned to recruit 2 posts of administrative cum finance assistants with a strong background in administrative procedures and finance handling regime. We would like you to place the following advertisement in your employment-classified section on the back page. Please display the advertisement on 25th January 2020 with diameter_____.

We are seeking qualified people with a strong professional background and work ethic and relevant experience to share in our values and enthusiasm towards eradicating Child labour.

Thanks

We stand for Human Rights Advocacy and protection.

Interview form

Interview form ....page 1,2

Applicant Name:_____ for position of _____

Age:_____ Nationality: _____ Proposed: _____

Work Experience

Relevance	1	2	3	4	5	Irrelevance

Relevance to the envisage experience:_____ Comments:_____

Level of experience

Special Skills

Education _____

Relevance	1	2	3	4	5	Irrelevance

Relevant to the organization requirements

Comments:_____

Level of education:_____

Field of expertise:_____

Interview Form Page 2

languages						
Desirable	1	2	3	4	5	Undesirable
Language	Excellent	Good	Satisfactory	fair	None	
Pashto						
Urdu						
English						
French						
Personality	Comments					
Motivation/ goal						
Conflict Resolution						
Leadership /team building						
Work Ethics						
Team spirit						
Taking initiative						
Physical stamina						
Communication Skills						
Cultural sensitivity						
Appearance						
Summary						
Additional Remarks						
Hired						
Not Hired						

Interviewer:_____

Date:_____

Rejection letter after interview

Date

Reforge non-profit

Address

Dear (_____)

As we have gone through your CV, but I am going to inform you that we choose to pursue those candidates whose experience and education background are matching with the job specification. If there is a match in the future, we will call you.

Wish you best of luck in a job hunt.

We appreciate your interest in our organization.

Sincerely,

HR manager

Acknowledgment of Application

Date:

From:

To:

We have received your application and CV and appreciate your interest in our organization. We regret to inform you, however, that the available position has been filled, and we cannot give your application further consideration at the moment.

Your application will be kept on file for future reference, if there is a suitable opportunity arise that match your qualification and experience

Sincerely yours,

HR manger: _____

An offer of Employment Letter

From: HR Manager   Ref:
Organization name   date:

To: Candidate Name:
Address:
Dear: (Name of candidate)

We are pleased to inform you that you have been offered the post of Project Coordinator. You are required to report to the office on_____. Your first point of contact is your immediate supervisor Mr. _____ Project Manager (Bonded labour). On your very first day, you will be given orientation and an employee manual to make your transition smooth.

Please, see HR Department to prepare certain papers. The HR department will give you all the papers that you are entitled to.

Thanks

HR Manager

Please confirm this offer letter by signing and return it back to the Human Resources Department

Candidate Signature_____ Date: _____

Offer Letter

Dear Mr Iqbal Shah

Passport No: _____

Country: _____

　Permanent address:

　urrent Address:

Subject: Letter of Appointment

On the basis of our telephonic interview and subsequent follow up we are pleased to offer your services on our Organization in the following terms:

Position: Office Manager/ Operation Manager

Duration: One year/ possibly extendable

Start Date: 20 Jan 2019

　　You will be governed by the service rules of this Organization as may be applicable to you from time to time. The Organization reserves the right to alter or modify its working hours or to increase them.

　　During the period of your employment, you will work honestly, faithfully, diligently and efficiently for the growth of the Organization.

We welcome you to our organization and look forward to your contribution to the growth of the company and yourself.

Thanks

Sincerely

Chief Executive Director

Organization

JOINING REPORT

Name		Date	
Department		Designation	
ID Passport No		NTN(National Tax No)	
Bank Account No		Bank and Branch	
Address			
Telephone/ Mobile No		Email Address	

EMPOYEE DECLARATION:
I solemnly declare that all the particulars mentioned above are true to my knowledge and belief.

SIGNATURE: _____ Date : _____

FOR OFFICE USE ONLY
EMPLOYEE ID: _____
LOCATION: _____
EMPLOYEE JOINED ON: _____
DEPARTMENT: _____
Document check list: _____
Security card form NTN Form: _____
Contract processed: _____

Offer letter/ Fact sheet' Interview form/ CV/ Educational Documents,

Appointment Letter, and Joining Letter, other particulars

sent to Finance Department: _____

Head of the Department. Approved by President: Director Human Resources

Office circular # _____

Employees' Profile (Excel Sheet)

Employee Name_____

PHOTO	Designation:	Project Manager Administration	Job Description
	Department		
	Hire Date:		
	Joining Date:		
SalaryDetails Particulars Amount Basic 13545.00 Medical Allowance 2550.00 Travel Allowance 1600.00 Education Allowance 1600.00 Conveyance Allowance 3100.00 HR 3375 00 Total 25770.00	Probation period:		
	Extension in probation:		
	Contract End Date		
	Date of Birth:		
	Employee ID:		
	Emergency Card No:		
	Mobile Phone:		
	Email Address:		
	Home Address:		
	Home Phone:		
	Qualification/ Education:		
	Experience:		
	Special Skills related to		
	Medical History:		

Welcome New Employee Letter

Dear Mr.

Welcome to our project team as Project Coordinator to gear it up.

I am delighted you are joining us as Project Coordinator. We are pleased that you have taken the decision to accept our offer. Our association will be a constant struggle to strengthen our relationship in a mutually beneficial way.

Here is some information that will make your transition smooth and also ensures you smartly pick up the points to have your seat and start working. We support you in any of your enquiry regarding your job.

Please, see your immediate supervisor as your first point of contact.

You are required to see HRD prepares some personnel files.

Yours Truly

Name:
Human Resources Manager

Employee Orientation Manual

Orientation aims to welcome new employee to know the working environment, feel comfortable at workplace, know the organization working behaviour, build rapport with colleagues and also to know his job descriptions very well and the seat where he/she has to perform or outside in the field if feasible a trip in the field. The immediate supervisor introduces the new employee to the organization ethics, vision, values and goals and objectives, and also the HR department keep the new employee abreast of all the tax laws, salary and benefits and if any paper to be filled in if the Department deems necessary.

Employees' handbook

Employees' handbook /Manual business card information Employees forms Insurance application Garage access keys welcome gift pack	Completed by	Date

Employee Fact Sheet

Employee name		Department	
Father's name		Designation	
Salary		Contact No	
Address		Marital Status	
Date of Birth		Date of Hiring	
Bank Account No		Branch/code	
Employee dependents			
Name	Relationship		Date of birth

I authorize the reefers to give you any or all information regarding my previous employment and pertinent information they may have , personal or otherwise

And release all parties from any liabilities that may result from furnishing same to you, I understand that giving any information about the Organization's finances, operation and or any other information that are confidential (unless officially authorized) to anyone including press, radio, TV and other media. It is organization's policy to treat all employees and applicants for employments without regard to race, religion, gender, age and handicapped. No discrimination is allowed on the above lines. I understand this policy and will adhere to it.

    I acknowledge that the Organization receives the right to amend or modify the policies contained in its policy manual at any time without prior notice. In understand that these policies are binding on me and I will adhere to them. These policies do not create any contractual obligation between the organization and its employees. I certify that the information that I declared is correct to the best of my knowledge and I understand that any holding back of information shall result in my dismissal.

Signature_____

References		
Name	Address	contact
1		
2		
3		

A Practical Guide to NGO and Project Management

Reference checking form

Employee Name ------------------ Department------------------

Employee ID -------------------- Joining date---------------------

Name----------------- Post applied for----------------

Reference1 ----------- Organization --------

Contact No ----------------

Questions to e asked

Did the employee work here?	
How long he worked in the organization?	
What was his/her position?	
What he /she did?	
What are his/her strengths?	
What are his/her weaknesses?	
What do you about his/her technical skills?	
What was his/her attitude towards colleagues?	
How did he/she handle conflicts?	
Why did he/she leave your organization?	
Would you rehire him/her?	

I Appreciate your cooperation, Thank you for the Comments on condidate

Previous job checking form

Employee name	Employee ID
if the candidate applied for a post	
Contact No	Address:
Organization	Contact No
Can you confirm that Mr./Miss---------------- worked here?	
In what capacity he/she worked here?	
And ending Please?	
What remuneration he/she drawn up? Starting please?	
And ending Please?	
Whether his/ her contract ended?	
I thank you for your cooperation.	
Comments if adverse:	

Probation evaluation

Name:_____Dept:_____

Date of joining: _____Date of Review:_____

Department: _____Supervisor: _____

Rating System

1= Unsatisfactory _____   2= Needs Improvement _____

Quality of Employee's work   _____

Comments_____

Honest & Reliable in carrying out instructions   _____

Comments_____

Punctuality/Attendance   _____

Comments_____

Employee involvement/participation in team effort _____

Comments_____

Attention to company policies and procedures   _____

Comments _____

Interpersonal relationships and communication with co-workers

Comments _____

Taking initiative to achieve goals and complete assignments

Comments _____

Responsiveness to changing work requirements

Comments_____

Work ethic   _____

Comments_____

Overall performance rating

Comments_____

Areas of Strength: ——————————————
_____

Areas of Improvement: ——————————————————

Employee's Comments:
_____

Date: _____   _____

　　　　Employee's Signature_____

For HR use only

Recommendations:_____
_____

_____
_____

Date_____Signature:_____

Probation extension letter

Employee Name

Address:

Date:

Sub: Extension of probation period

Dear {employee name}

We are going to inform you that your probation period has been extended to another 3 months starting from your current probation expiry date.

Your supervisor will give you a written letter stating the areas of improvement.

HR manager

Please confirm this extension if you want to continue with the organization and return it to HR

Employee Signature: _____ Date: _____

Employment letter after probation

Confirmation of employment letter after successful probation period

Dear, {employee name}

We are pleased to inform you that you have successfully qualified your probation period.

Based on our assessment, we are confirming your employment as our full staff member and you are now in our permanent employees' pole and claim all the benefits thereof.

Your compensation as permanent employee comes as follow

Gross salary: _____

Benefits: _____

Deduction: _____

Net salary: _____

Please confirm it.

Yours sincerely,

HR Manager

As per recruitment policy, I confirm the terms and condition that post carries.

Signature   Date: …………………………..

Promotion Letter

January 22, 2019

Mr..................

Associate project Manager

Dear,

Due to your good performance, proactive attitude, cooperative working spirit, we are pleased to announce that you are promoted to associate project manager to assist project Manager in her work. The new post requires a lot of zeal and tact and responsibility on part of you and trust that you will do to the best of your ability and potential. Please see project manager immediately. Your new compensation structure is as follows:

Compensation Head	Existing	Incremented	total
Basic DA			
Conveyance Allowance			
Medical Reimbursement			
Food Allowance			
Change of Assignment Allowance			
Subtotal of Annual Salary			
Employer contribution to PF			
Annual Total			

The raise in your salary would be applicable from January 1st, 2019. Your next compensation review will come up in September 2019. Please see HR manager as your first point of contact.

Yours Sincerely,

Manager HR:_____

Employee benefit survey

"Please fill it and return it to human resources department"

Survey questions	Employees
Are you satisfied with your current benefits structure?	
What should increased or decreased?	
Does the leave structure is satisfactory?	
Does the general health plan is satisfactory?	
Are you satisfied with specific health policies?	
Are you satisfied with on the job trainings?	
Are you satisfied with your professional growth?	
Are you satisfied with your promotion policy?	
Are you satisfied with your current salary structure?	
Does the organization provide for long term?	
Are you satisfied with the organization social policy?	
Additional comments:	

Employee's Name:_____

Department:_____

Signature:_____

Employee Performance Review

Employee Name	Employee ID	Department	Designation
Supervisor Name		Department	Designation

Supervisor's comments			
Excellent	Good	Satisfactory	Training needed
Technical abilities			
Current job skill level			Technical ability
Understanding of SOPs			Technical comprehension level
Communication level			Articulateness
Performance			
Punctuality			Leave record
Initiation level			Quality of work
Responsibility			Independence
Organized			Creative
Delegation			Work knowledge
Team spirit			
Attitude towards colleagues			Cooperation
Building team techniques			Tact
Leadership			Obedience
Additional comments			
Next review goals:-			

Employee signature:_____ Date:_____
Supervisor signature:

Employee self-evaluation

Answer the following questions by checking the appropriate box to the right. After you have finished answering each question, total the number of checked boxes in each column Multiply the total of each column by the severity factor for that category. Add together the total of each column. This is your evaluation score. The higher the score, the better will be the understanding of Reforgenonprofit, its structure and your role in it.

	Below Average 1	Satisfactory 2	Above average 3	Superior 4
I know my job description.				
I know who my supervisor is and what he or she is responsible for				
I feel my workload is too heavy.				
I feel I can discuss my problems with my superior.				
I know what my benefits are.				
I feel that I am a part of a productive work team.				
I always know what my daily and weekly goals are.				
I know what the long-term goals of the organization are.				
I know what the organizational structure of the organization is.				
I feel I have had enough training to perform my job.				
Multiply the responses by each column's severity factor.				
Add the results for your total audit score				

Increment Letter

Dear, {employee name}

Congratulations.

The review has taken place this _____ on _____ and we are pleased to inform you that you salary has been incremented as follows:

Existing Benefits	Incremented	Total
	Total	

Please sign in and return.

HR manager

Name: _____

Signature of the employee

Regards,

Office Circular Note

Organization Name and logo

Address:
Ref OCO NO: Date:
Subject: raise in salary

We are hereby informing you all concerned that we are raising the salaries of the following employees to be effective from 01st March 2012.

Name _____

Designation _____   Present gross salary _____

Proposed salary _____

Submitted to Chief Executive Officer and approval granted by the department of human resources management.

HR department

Approved by CEO _____

Employee status form

Employee Name_____ Employee Code_____

Job title Department_____

Location_____

Status change effective from:_____

title change Current title Raised:_____

title:_____

transfer   transfer from _____

                              transfer to_____

Department change _____Current dept _____new dept_____

Salary change _____Current salary_____ Revised salary_____

Change in personal   information_____

Remarks:_____

Processing of employee status form

Initiated by_____ Checked by_____ verified by_____ approved by_____

Date _____Date _____Date_____

HUMAN RESOURCES DEPARTMENT CHECKLIST

Database updated, Department head notified_____ Director / Manager Human Resources

Personal file updated finance department informed_____   Approved by:_____

Employee Status Report

Employee information				
Employee Name		Employee ID		
Department		Manager		
Report start date		Report end date		
Long term goals	Due date		Progress	
Accomplishments				
Concerns				

Payslip letter

NAME
Executive Director

Date:

Salary Certificate

This to certify that **[EMPLOYEE NAME]** employed with our company as a **Social Organizer** From _____ has received a consolidate salary of Rs.25, 000 per month from _____ to _____ .

During her tenure, we found her to be hard-working, diligent and sincere. Her services were found to be extremely satisfactory.

Regards,
NAME
Executive Director
[Organization's Name]

Disciplinary Steps

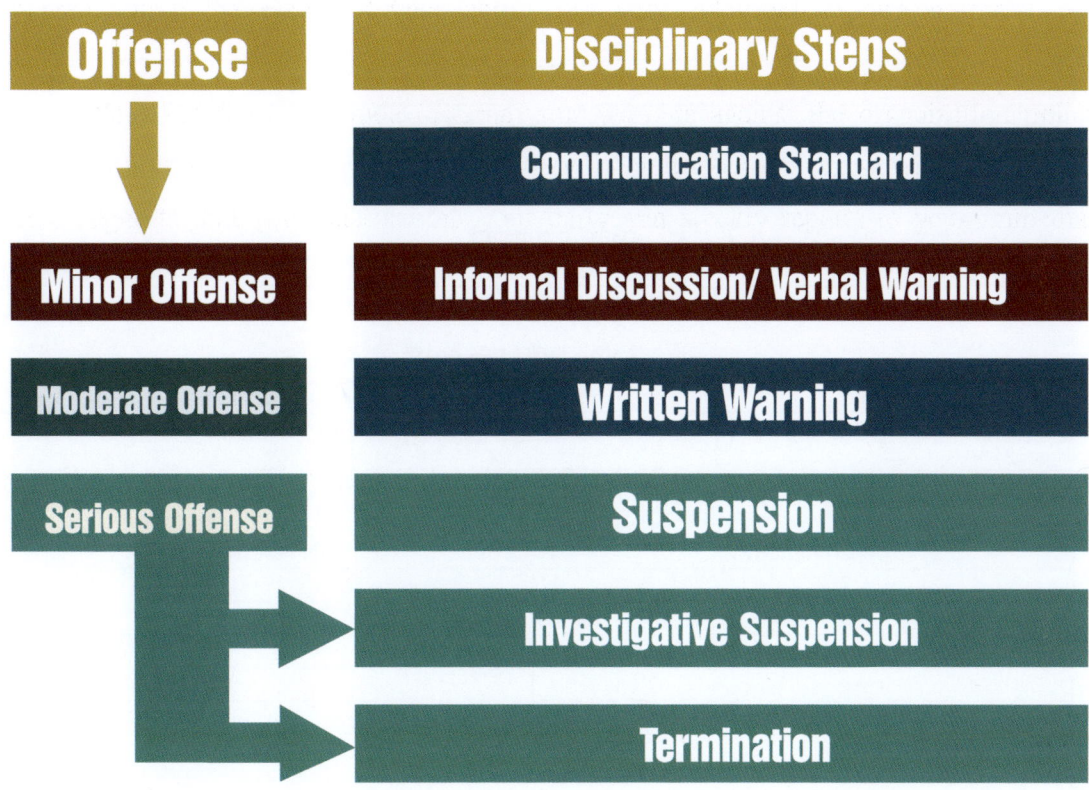

Training Need Assessment

Knowledge		Skills		Motivation		Disciplinary issues	

Current skill level of efficiency and effectiveness:
Current staff doing and what required of them to do well and their desire to acquire new or upgrade existing skills to do efficiently and effectively.

Gap Identified

Job description	Skill Required	Department

What staff lack? tick boxes

Gap identified	Current skill level	Required skill level to perform better

Departmental Review

Department Head	Skill Assessment
Training needed	
Training	Cost

HR Manager_____

Written reprimand

Dear _____

Your immediate supervisor has a complain written against you which states that you are not up to the task and did not submit your daily and weekly reports on time.

Your indifferent attitude towards your work is against the organization policy. Because it is in your job description that you will abide by the rules and will comply with; which suggests that you must submit your daily and weekly reports to your immediate supervisor on time.

hereby inform you to take notice of this and submit your reports on time so that a smooth congenial working relationship may take place.

Sincerely,

CEO : _____

Disciplinary Action Records

Employee Name _____ Joining date _____ Department _____
Supervisor _____

For Human Resources Record

Violation #1	Warning Notice	Employee Intimation
Breach of policies	Date:	Decision By:
1	Verbal Notice:	
2	Written reprimand:	Goal of disciplinary action:
3	Dismissal:	
4	Termination:	
Violation #1	Warning Notice	Employee Intimation
Breach of policies	Date:	Decision By:
1	Verbal Notice:	
2	Written reprimand:	Goal of disciplinary action:
3	Dismissal:	
4	Termination:	
Violation #1	Warning Notice	Employee Intimation
Breach of policies	Date:	Decision By:
1	Verbal Notice:	
2	Written reprimand:	Goal of disciplinary action:
3	Dismissal:	
4	Termination:	

1. Employee's remarks notice _____

2. Employee's remarks notice _____

Employee's remarks notice : _____

Final Warning Letter

Date:

To: (Employee)

We have previously notified you of certain problems in your performance as an employee, which are still continuing. Continuing with such an attitude could result in your immediate dismissal without further warning.

Sincerely,

Verbal Warning Letter

Ref No:

Date:

To

Employee name:

Subject: Disciplinary Meeting

Sub: <u>Absenteeism</u>

We held a meeting on (Date), attended by (Employee's name), me, and a third party, (Name of the third party). At the meeting, it was brought to the employee's attention that his /her tardiness record was unacceptable as he/she had been late 6 times during the past 3 weeks. The employee was warned that if she/he tardiness continued, further corrective disciplinary action, up to and including dismissal, would be taken.

The employee was intimated that this was a formal written warning and that his/her personnel file will be updated.

Signature: _____

Notice of unsatisfactory Performance

Reference no: Date:

To: (Employee)

We held a meeting with your immediate supervisor and we came to know that there are certain performance-related issues that need to be resolved properly and require due diligence and care on the part of you.

We hope that those omissions and commissions of actions will not be repeated. Continuous carelessness may cause serious repercussions.

Guiding you to success
Sincerely,

Show Cause Letter

Date: 12th January 2019

Dear:

Re: **SHOW CAUSE LETTER**

It has been reported to the Human Resource Manager on Wednesday, 6th January 2019 that at approximately 11.30 a.m. on 1st January 2019 that you failed repeatedly to submit your field reports on time.

You are hereby suspended for full pay for 8 days and you should report in writing to the authority concerned.

This suspension may not deem to be a punishment. Your alleged misconduct will be investigated further.

If you failed to submit a written explanation, then the decision may go against you without any further written or verbal notice to you.

....

(Signature of CEO)_____

Signature of Human Resources Manager_____

Suspension Letter

Date:_____

Employee Name :_____
Dear: _____

This letter is to inform you that you are hereby suspended from your job without pay for _____ working days, commencing _____. This disciplinary action is being taken based on the following policy breaches.

1. Policy Breach 1
2. Breach 2

Your actions are causes of severe breaches of policy no_____ and _____ as written in the employee manual and therefore, call for disciplinary action to be taken against you. As your personnel and disciplinary records show that HRD has warned you for the same misconduct 2 times in the past. We are taking the following disciplinary action as a corrective measure.

Suspension without pay for 10 consecutive working days beginning 07-03-2019.

Sincerely,
HRM

Relieving Letter

REFERENCE:)_____ Date:_____

    The resignation letter dated of Mr._____ has been accepted by the Chief Executive Officer with effect from Monday on_____. Henceforth, the employee is no longer at service to the organization and all the benefits are, therefore, stand withdrawn.

    You are hereby informed to submit all the belonging of this organization including your ID CARD.

HR MANAGER

Receipt of Written Reprimand

I acknowledge receipt of this written reprimand. My acknowledgement does not necessarily signify my agreement with its contents. I understand that a copy of this written reprimand will be placed in my official personnel file. I also understand that I have the right to prepare a written response that will be attached to the originally written reprimand in my file.

Signature: _____

Employee Name: _____

Date: _____

Resignation Accepted

Dear Concern,

It is with deep regret, that we accept your resignation as [**position/Designation**]of the [**organization**].

We appreciate all of the pain ad efforts you took and put to get the job done as a[**Position/Designation**]

Very truly,

Organization

CEO

Termination Letter

Date

Employee Name

Dear:

We are intimating you through this letter that your services are being terminated effective from _____, the organization owes some severance pay that you are entitled to get as we agreed on your joining this organization.

      Regular wages Rs:000000

This severance that you are getting is our acknowledgement of the services that you rendered to the organization in the capacity of Associate Project manager for the last_____ years.

Sincerely Yours.
HRM

Employee's signature: _____

Date:

Termination Notice

Every action has an opposite reaction. **Reforgenonprofit** has repeatedly made you aware that a change was needed in [Matter], no improvement has been apparent over the last [**DAYS**].

Your lack of action leaves us no choice but to terminate your employment with **Reforgenonprofit** effective from [**DATE**].

Your future outside **Reforgenonprofit** is dependent upon you recognizing it. Learn from your mistakes to avail the chance to have all that you need to have.

"Life begins at the end of your comfort zone"

Wishing you a very best luck in future

HR MANAGER_____
CHIEF EXECUTIVE_____

CHAPTER NINE:

Reporting to Donors- Formats and Procedures:

Reporting to donors is almost mandatory on every organization as to check whether or not the objectives against the funds are being achieved. During the implementation phase of PCM reports are prepared to check progress on project objectives. Daily, weekly, fortnightly, monthly, quarterly, six-monthly or yearly reports are prepared by the project staff to make the management and donors aware of the progress on project objectives. Down to top approach is adopted in the preparation of these reports. As field staff prepare reports for their immediate supervisors and the supervisors, in turn, prepare a report back to NGO headquarter. The management in headquarters reports to the donor according to agreed TORs in the funding agreement. Reports usually ensure to share information, experiences, promote accountability, adding insights and analysis into the problems, gauging progress and failure, thought-provoking to plan a new if failures occur.

Types of Reports

There are usually two types of reports; one is called a narrative report and the other one is the financial report.

Narrative Reports:

These reports are prepared by non-finance staff as per their schedule activities in the field or office and are narrative in the sense that describes the progress of the project towards achieving its objectives. These reports are prepared on set formats according to the nature of activities as per schedule or job description by the headquarter written in the log frame. These reports are usually submitted to immediate supervisors in the field branch or to headquarter directly. From these reports planned versus actual progress on a project, objectives are measured is gauged. So the timeline of activities in the field is checked, planned versus actual activities are measured through these reports.

Financial Repor

The field finance or administrative staffs usually prepare these reports for the NGO's management back in headquarter to check that activities planned are within the stipulated budget released for the field branch office/ project area office. These reports are usually called donor budget monitoring reports. These financial are submitted by the NGO headquarter to the donor to gauge and measure that activities timeline is followed within a stipulated budget for each activity

Non-profit/NGO daily Progress Report

NGO daily progress is recorded on a given format according to the nature of activities aimed at achieving project objectives, purpose and overall goal as set forth in the log frame. These reports record daily progress by measuring objectively verifiable indicators and in itself is a source of verification for these measurable indicators on the project objective. So everyone who prepares reports must be proficient in narrative report writing and know his or her job description in clear terms that what his/her activities are going to achieve in terms of progress on project objectives. They must know project objectives and purpose so as to check whether or not they are heading towards achieving project objectives keeping in view activities timeline. In the reports, they also mention if there is an incident, risks, issue or problem they are facing in carrying out their activities. If such circumstances exist, the staff report carried it forward in that written progress report to his/her immediate supervisor and if possible propose strategies to address issues and mitigate risks. So the supervisors note it down in the issue or risk log and propose strategies to mitigate and also check progress on issue status that whether or not the issue was resolved, pending or in progress. So every progress report must have columns for activities to be undertaken, objectives that will be achieved and the strategies adopted for achieving objectives. In case there is a failure of activities the columns specified will indicate the date, failed activity, the reason for failure and proposed strategies for mitigation . **(see the format in chapter nine on project reports).** The staff will also indicate in his/her report if an activity is going to be redundant or no longer needed, and cannot produce results.

The supervisor may report it to the NGO headquarter, and after analysis, the management reports it to the donor and obtained written permission that the strategy or activity is no longer effective as planned to be carried and amendment in the activity log is needed in order to adjust it. If the budget is affected by the amendment in the activity, the project manager or management in the NGOs head quarter discuss this with the donor, and if the donor agrees on the amendment and change, written permission is sought from the donor to do so.

(See chapter nine on project reports for such a request)

Tips on Writing Effective Progress Reports

The SMART

criterion is to be applied for writing effective project progress reports:

SMART criterion for effective project report writing
by Iqbal Shah

S — Reports must be specific short, simple and straightforward and that they convey the message concisely. Reports convey progress on objectives that are set forth in the long frame matrix

M — Reports are measurable in terms of achieving results on project objectives. Repors describes the results, outputs according to inputs given. So reports measure the progress on projects objectives. Reports record acual versyus planned results

A — Logframe sets forth what are attainable add accuracy to it. Analytical Insights are added to reports to further capitalize on them

R — The material in the report must be strictly relevant and realistic and up to the mark. Reports are records of activities undertaken and the results achieved strategies implied and gaps risk issues identified and mitigating strategies formulated and failures noted.

T — Reports are conveyed in timely manner. They are time bound according to project activities schedule and the results they will achieve. As every project is time bound, so are reports. Every activity that is undertaken, must have correspondent result there of and recorded in reports.

Plan of operation

Activities	
1	
2	
3	
Expected results	
1	
2	
3	
Schedule	
Person in charge	
Implementer	
Means needed	
1	
2	
3	
cost	
remarks	

Reported by: ———————— Reported to: ————————————————————

Daily Progress Report

Name of person reporting	Designation	Report date
Core activities completed	Output of activities/target achieved	Strategies implied
Activities remained incomplete	Reasons for failure of activities	Proposed remedies to complete the remaining activities

Signature of official:_____   Received by:_____

A Practical Guide to NGO and Project Management

Site Visit Report page1

Project Details

Organization and logo	Project Title
	Project Number:
	Document Owner:

Visit Details		Project Name	
		Donor	
		Contact Details	
		Project Manager	
		Date of	
		Time of visit	
		Location for Site Visit	
		Hours/ duration	
Document Details			
	Document	Name	Site visit report
Review detail			
	Review list	Name	

Site visit report page 2

Recommendations

page 2 Site visit
Current Work
Describe your recommendations on the work that has been undertaken
1. Vigorous mass campaign
2. Meeting bonded labour
3. Meeting employers
Future Work
Describe your recommendations on future work that may be undertaken
1. Continuous vigorous mass campaign
2. Continuous involving of line government department to implement labour laws
Budget Utilization

Describe costs related to the site visit

Resource type	Budget items	Duration
Total		

Site visit report page 3

Primary Objective:---
------- eradicating bonded labour: --------------------------
Current Issue(s):--
Employers (kiln owners) not cooperating: --------------------------
Proposed Solution: ---
involving government labour and other line departments.

Project Tasks & Assumptions

task Description	Assigned to
1 Mobilizing community	Mobilizer
2 meeting line government department	Project manager
3 Meeting community leaders	Project coordinator
4 mass awareness campaign. developing flyer	Project manager

Overview of tasks   Description   Assumptions

Describe the assumption you have related to this project
1. Line department Involvement   2. community leaders involvement
Task Status   Completed Tasks
Describe completed tasks

Task description	Status	Assigned to
Community mobilization	In progress	Mobilizer
Mass awareness campaign	In progress	Mobilizer
Human rights flyer development	completed	PM

Daily Progress Report

Name of person reporting	Designation	Report date
Core activities completed	Output of activities/target achieved	Strategies implied
Activities remained incomplete	Reasons for failure of activities	Proposed remedies to complete the remaining activities

Signature of official:_____   Received by: _____

A Practical Guide to NGO and Project Management

Project lessons learn report

Project name: "Say no to debt bondage labour in the brick kiln industies"
Department:_____ Document Owner :_____
Focus Area:_____ Project Organization role:_____
Product Of the process

Version	Date	Author	Change Description

Project Success	Factors That Supported Success
Brick kiln workers trained in other livelihood alternatives	The training process was made interactive and practical
Employer and line government department were made to take note of the fact that law prohibits such kind of labour and labourers were trained to voice their opinion in determining minimum wages and unions are in place now	Training in labour human rights line department involvement and their pledge to eradicate the menace by enforcing the law of the land regarding labours' welfare.
Children are now at school	Informal schools led to pave the way for children to the formal schooling system
Other Notable Project Successes	
Project Success	Factors That Supported Success
Workers are now in better place to voice their opinion through their own active union	Labour unions were formed
Health education made the workers led to their better health conditions	Informal training in health education'
Mother and child health were fostered through training by existing lady health worker project staff	Training in informal health education

Project Name: 'Say no to debt bondage labour in brick kiln industries" Project Highlights
Top 3 Significant Project Successes:

A Practical Guide to NGO and Project Management

Project lessons learned continue..Page2

Project Shortcomings and Solutions:_____

Project Shortcoming	Recommended Solutions
Area was too much far flung and reaching out to it was difficult	Project staff were made available in the field branch offices and villages were made into clustered and each cluster had its own staffs
Resistance from employers	local leaders must take interest and law enforcing agencies must take note of any violation that occurs.
lack of interest on the parts of local leaders and law enforcing agencies	

Project approval ─────────────────
Prepared by:_____ Project Manager_____
Approved by:_____
Project Sponsor

Project Narrative Report page 2

Activities undertaken
Text here
Amendments in Activities
Text here
Proposed Amendments in activities
Text here
Results Achieved
Text here
Issued raised
Text here
litigating strategies implied
Text here
Community Proposed Amendments
Text here
Field Staff Remarks
Text here
Conclusions
Text here
Financial Report For the period
See Annexure Attached

By Iqbal Shah

Budget Monitoring Report

Financial report		Project: Bonded Labour			1st Oct 2019 to March 2020		
Code	Budget Items	Total Grant	Budget to Oct	Actual spent	Variance	% budget variance	Remarks
	Administration Personnel						
	Project manager						
	Project Coordinator						
	Social Organizers						
	Supporting Staff						
	Sub-Total						
	Office Running Cost						
	Utilities						
	Telephone -emails-Postages						
	Rent						
	Equipment repair /maintenance						
	Fuel						
	Vehicle Repair						
	Office supply						
	Bank charges						
	Sub-Total						
	Total Administration Cost						
	Assets cost						
	Desk / Chairs/ tables						
	Computer/ laptop						
	Total capital Cost						
	Programme Running Cost						
	Training						
	Field visits						
	Monitoring and Documentation						
	Total programme cost						
	Grand Total						

Change of Assignment Log

S#	Request Title	Request Date	Originator	Assigned to	Response date	Status	Close date
1							
2							
3							
4							
5							
6							
7							

ISSUE LOG (Excel)

Date Reported	Issue No	Issue description	Reported by	Actions proposed	Actions taken	Due Date	Priority	Status

Activities Schedule Log

"Say no to bonded labour in brick kiln industries"

Activities	Time line/ Duration	Completion date	Assigned to
Gathering information about bonded labour in brick kiln industries (especially child bonded labour), conducting surveys through field visits, questionnaire distribution, interviews, and getting background knowledge from line department as labour department, ministry of industries and divisions.	One month (January 2016)	31 January 2016	Programme manager
Developing the initial project proposal by analyzing the data collected on above lines.	10 Days (Feb 2016)	February 2016	Grant Writer
Mobilizing the community through face to face meeting with people in command of the situation, such as line departments, relevant law enforcing agencies, ministries, divisions, wings, industrialists, and the primary and stakeholders (labour in brick kiln industries). Implying rights based strategies among the laborers.	One month starting mid February to mid March	Feb 12 to March 12- 2016	Field Officer (community mobilizer)
Devising strategies to make these brick kiln laborers getting other skills as alternatives to make them more skillful and less dependent on these industries, and making them more independent to remove their dependency syndrome on these industries, making them seek wealth management techniques through practical means and resources.	One month, starting March 15th to April 15th	15 March to April 15th--2016	Programme manager / Field Coordinator

Note down main activities from activity log from log fame by categorizing them into primary and secondary activities to avoid omission of main activities, keeping dependency of activities as completing one and leading to next level of activities and avoiding doubling and overburdening staff at the cost of other.

Resource scheduling log

code	Activities/ Resources	Means required	Unit cost	Total unit cost	Quarter 1	Quarter 2	Quarter 3	Quarter 4	Total project cost
	Community mobilization	Logistics support							
		Vehicle cost							
		Diesel							
		Petrol							
		CNG							
		Repairs							

Report prepared by: _____

Reporting period: _____

Field Staff Risk/Issues Identification Log

Reported by _____ Reported to _____

Date	Risks identified	Issues identified	Mitigating strategies	Status
				In progress
				Completed
				Postpone

A Practical Guide to NGO and Project Management

Field Staff Monthly Report

Reported by_____ Reported to_____ Date submitted_____

for the month of _____

Week first	Objective achieved	Risk identified	Issues raised
Activity 1			
Activity 2			
Week first			
Activity 1			
Activity 2			
Week first			
Activity 1			
Activity 2			
Week first			
Activity 1			
Activity 2			
Failure of activities			
Activities	Reasons for failure	Mitigating strategies devised	status
Activity 1			
Activity 2			
Proposed amendments in activities	Activities proposed		
Activity 1			
Activity 2			

Supervisor comments:

Activities	Supervisor comments	Accepted / rejected
Activity 1		
Activity 2		

By Iqbal Shah

Field Staff Monthly Report

Supervisor's remarks	Reasons for rejection	
Activity 1		
Activity 2		
For project Manager	**Reason for rejection or acceptance**	
Activity 1		
Activity 2		
For Management	**Reason for rejection or acceptance**	
Report to donor	**Budgetline amendments**	**Accepted /rejected**
Activity 1		
Activity 2		
For donor	**Donor reason for acceptance**	**Donor reasons for rejection**
Activity 1		
Activity 2		
Partial acceptance		
Activity 1		
Activity 2		

Action Plan Corrective Measures (Excel Sheet)

Problem	
Issue	
Failure	
Causes	
Related department	
Person Reporting	
Reported to	
Task assigned to	
Strategies implied	

CHAPTER TEN

Project proposal writing techniques

A guide to project proposal writing

What is a project proposal?

A project proposal is a written document consisting of strategies/operational plan to address an issue/problem in a given duration/time with a specific goal, purpose and deliverable results with inputs (means and budget) given to undertake activities by mobilizing means and resources/cost/budget/human and otherwise.

Project Proposal main points

Project proposal consists of the following:
Project title, target people and target area
Introduction to organization
Project brief
Problem statement
Benefits to the target people
Objective statement
Project main activities
Outputs
Monitoring
Evaluation
Sustainability of the project
Staffs capabilities
Project budget

Project proposal main points

See Diagram No 45:

Project proposal main points	
Project	Title: Project Name, Target people, Target area
Summary	Summary / Project brief (a brief introduction to the main points of the project)
Objective Analysis	How the project is going to address the problem? Design, rationale, strategy, analysis and operational plan
Activities	Activities (main activities are noted down to achieve project objectives)
Means/ Resources	means and cost (resource are gathered and budget is prepared)
M&E Plan	Monitoring and evaluation plan is prepared as to check progress on planned versus actual activites one the implementation gets started.
Sustainability Factors	project short and log term benefits to the target people are taken into account
Budget	Itemized budget is prepared to undertake activities to achieve project objectives

Bibliography and References:

1- (World Bank, 2001).
2- (Schmidt and Take 1997).
3- Geneva Convention.
4- Ali Mostashari, An introduction to non-governmental organization management, 2005]
5- Project Cycle Management handbook by European Commission, May 1999
6- Project Cycle Management handbook by European Commission, May 1999" **[6],**
7- Robert Chambers (1992) and Andrea Cornwall, Irene Guijt and Alice Welboum (1993),
8- Chambers, R, (1980), **Rural Development: Putting the Last First** Harlow, England
9- United Nations Population Fund defines a project in "Capacity Building of NGOs in Post Conflict Situations" http://www.unfpa.org/women/docs/manual4-ngos.pdf

Printed in Poland
by Amazon Fulfillment
Poland Sp. z o.o., Wrocław